Power-up Trainer for the TOEFL® ITP

TOEFL is a registered trademark of Educational Testing Service(ETS).
This publication is not endorsed or approved by ETS.

Mark D. Stafford
Chizuko Tsumatori

CENGAGE
Learning™

CENGAGE
Learning™

Power-up Trainer for the TOEFL® ITP [Text Only]

Mark D. Stafford and Chizuko Tsumatori

© 2010 Mark D. Stafford/Chizuko Tsumatori

Photo Credits:
cover: © AFLO

ISBN: 978-4-86312-417-2

Cengage Learning K.K.
No 2 Funato Building 5th Floor
1-11-11 Kudankita, Chiyoda-ku
Tokyo 102-0073
Japan

Tel: 03-3511-4392
Fax: 03-3511-4391

はしがき

　ご存知のように TOEFL®は、英語を母国語としない者が、英語圏の大学・大学院へ留学する際に、必要な英語運用能力を有しているかどうかを測るテストとして、すっかり定着しています。その証拠に、英語圏の多くの大学・大学院で、留学生に一定の TOEFL®スコアを求めています。

　しかし、TOEFL®で高スコアを獲得するのは、けっして易しくありません。日本の学生が、このハードルをクリアするには、特にどのような点を鍛える必要があるのでしょうか。

　第一に挙げられるのは「語彙力」です。大学・大学院の授業を理解可能かを試すために、TOEFL®ではアカデミックな用語が多数出題されます。しかし、日本で暮らす多くの日本人にとって、英語の学術的用語に触れる機会は少ないのが実情です。この点が、どうしても大きな壁となってしまいます。

　そして、もうひとつ、長い英文を読み、あるいは聞いて、すばやく的確に理解する力を鍛えなければいけません。同じように人気の高いテストである TOEIC®と比較しても、TOEFL®では、より長い文章への読解力・聴解力が求められます。

　本書では、この2点を重点的に鍛えることにしました。

　各ユニットの構成は、英文パッセージを読み（奇数ユニット）、あるいはダイアログ・モノローグを聞き（偶数ユニット）ながら、そこに含まれる学術的・専門的語彙を習得することを柱としています。英文は、TOEFL®の出題傾向を分析し、自然科学・社会科学系の内容、さらに大学生活上の日常会話などを扱っています。

　また、語彙力の強化方法については、あえて英語で語義を理解させるアクティビティを盛り込みました。本書が対象とする TOEFL® ITPで、500点以上を目指すには、そうした練習が不可欠だからです。

　文法についても、各ユニットの後半で、要点を簡単におさらいした後、模擬問題に挑戦できるようになっています。

　本書の活用目的は、さまざまでしょうが、留学を考えている人は、本書をその具体的な第一歩としてください。また、そうでない人にとっても、本書が、より高度でアカデミックな英語に親しむきっかけになれば幸いです。

編集部

Contents

本書の使い方

Pre-test / Post-test

両テストともに、問題数は32問、受験時間約30分のミニ模擬試験となっています。
問題の内訳は、次のとおりです。

Section 1	Part A	4問	
	Part B	4問	13分
	Part C	4問	
Section 2	Structure	5問	7分
	Written Expression	5問	
Section 3		10問	10分

Pre-testは学習前の実力測定に、Post-testは12ユニット学習後の達成度チェックにご活用ください。
両テストの音声は、教師用CDにのみ収録されています。トラック番号を示すマークが 🎧 となっているのでご注意ください。

ユニット構成

TOEFL® ITPのSection 3 対策となる長文読解を奇数ユニットで、Section 1 対策のリスニングを偶数ユニットで学習します。Section 2 で問われる文法知識については、全ユニットで取り上げています（☞TOEFL® ITPの詳細はp. 6-7 を参照）。

Try the TOEFL Test!
TOEFL® ITP形式の練習問題に挑戦します。
奇数ユニットでは 300〜400 wordsの長文読解に取り組み、偶数ユニットではSection 1 のPart A, B, C それぞれの問題に取り組みます。
また、全ユニットで、Section 2 形式の問題にも取り組みます。

Vocabulary Check!
TOEFL受験の際、大きな壁となるのが語彙です。学術的な用語、専門用語をしっかりと学習します。

Building Reading Skills!(奇数ユニット)
読解力を磨くための、各種アクティビティに挑戦します。

Building Listening Skills!(偶数ユニット)
ディクテーションなど、聴解力を磨くためのアクティビティに挑戦します。

Speaking(偶数ユニット)
英文の音読やロールプレイに取り組みながら、英語をアウトプットする力を養います。

One Point Grammar
Section 2 で頻出、あるいは長文読解に必要不可欠な文法項目を説明。要点を絞った解説で、文法知識のブラッシュアップを行います。

TOEFL® ITP とは？

I. テストの概要

TOEFL®（Test of English as a Foreign Language）とは、アメリカのEducational Testing Serviceが作成した、英語運用能力を測るためのテストで、世界の180カ国で実施されています。そのスコアは、アメリカやカナダ、イギリスなどの大学で、英語を母国語としない入学希望者の英語力を測る指標として活用されています。

2010年1月現在、日本で受験できるのはTOEFL® iBTとTOEFL® ITPの2種類[※1]です。

TOEFL® iBTのiBTは、Internet-Based Testの略です。つまり、インターネット上で実施されるテストです。一方、TOEFL® ITPはInstitutional Testing Program、つまり、大学などの団体受験用のTOEFL®です。解答は、紙のマークシートに行います。

この2種類のテストは、実施方法だけでなく、テスト内容も異なります。本書が対象としているのは、TOEFL® ITPのほうです。TOEFL® ITPは過去に実施されたTOEFL® PBT[※2]の問題を再利用して構成されています。そのため、そのスコアは公式なものではありませんが、TOEFL® iBTのスコアと高い相関関係にあり、多くの教育機関で、プレイスメントテスト、成績評価の手段として活用されています。

II. テスト構成

テストは大きく、①リスニングセクション、②文法セクション、③リーディングセクションに分けられ、①と②については、さらに複数のパートに分けられます。問題数やテスト時間とともに下表にまとめているので、ご覧ください。

	Section 1: Listening Comprehension			Section 2: Structure and Written Expression		Section 3: Reading Comprehension
	Part A	Part B	Part C	Part A	Part B	
問題数	30問	8問	12問	15問	25問	50問
問題形式	4択					
制限時間	約35分			25分		55分

それぞれのセクション、パートの詳細は次のとおりです。

◆Section 1: Listening Comprehension

Part A

A→B、もしくはA→B→Aという2人の人物の短い会話を聞き、その内容に関する設問に答えます。会話と設問は音声のみで、テスト冊子には印刷されていません。4つの選択肢A～Dだけが印刷されています。音声は一度だけ流れます。

2人の人物の長めの会話を聞き、その内容を問う設問に答えます。各会話文に3～5題の設問が設定されています。Part A同様、会話文と設問は音声だけで、冊子には印刷されていません。選択肢のみが印刷されています。音声が流れるのも1回のみです。会話の内容は、大学生活に関連したものが主に出題されます。

Part C

1人の人物による説明や講義を聞き、その内容を問う設問に答えます。出題される説明・講義は4つで、それぞれに3～5題の設問がつきます。説明・講義、そして設問は音声のみで、選択肢だけがテスト冊子に印刷されています。音声は一度だけ流れます。話される内容は、大学教授による講義や、授業のオリエンテーションなどが多く出題されます。

◆Section 2: Structure and Written Expression

Structure

空所を含む短い英文が提示され、その空所に入る適切な語句を選択肢A～Dから選び出します。

Written Expression

4個所に下線が引かれた短い英文が提示され、4つのうち文法上の誤りを含むものを選び出します。

◆Section 3: Reading Comprehension

長い英文が提示され、その内容を問う設問に答えます。出題されるパッセージは5つ。それぞれに10問程度の設問がついています。パッセージの内容は、アメリカの大学の一般教養課程レベルの人文科学・社会科学・自然科学的なものになります。

III. スコア

TOEFL® ITPのスコアは、310～677の範囲で算出されます。
まず、各セクションのスコアが、正答数をもとに次の範囲で算出されます。この3つのスコアを合計して、10倍し、さらに3で割ったのが総スコアです。

Section 1	31～68
Section 2	31～68
Section 3	31～67

例）Section 1が45点、Section 2が40点、Section 3が40点の場合
　　（45+40+40）× 10 ÷ 3 = 417 ※小数点以下は四捨五入
　　よって、総スコアは417点です。

※1: TOEFL® ITPはさらに、難易度別に、Level 1とLevel 2に分類されます。通常の難易度のものがLevel 1で、本書はこちらを対象としています。Level 2はLevel 1よりも易しい内容です。
※2: TOEFL® PBT（Paper-Based Test）は、現在日本国内では実施されていません。

Section 1
Listening Comprehension

 Track 02-06

In this section of the test, you will have an opportunity to demonstrate your ability to understand conversations and talks in English. There are three parts to this section with special directions for each part. Answer all the questions on the basis of what is stated or implied by the speakers you hear. Do **NOT** take notes or write in your test book at any time. Do **NOT** turn the pages until you are told to do so.

Part A

Directions: In Part A, you will hear short conversations between two people. After each conversation, you will hear a question about the conversation. The conversations and questions will not be repeated. After you hear a question, read the four possible answers in your test book and choose the best answer. Then, on your answer sheet, find the number of the question and fill in the space that corresponds to the letter of the answer you have chosen.

Here is an example.
On the recording, you will hear:

In your test book, you will read: (A) He doesn't like the painting either.
                                     (B) He doesn't know how to paint.
                                     (C) He doesn't have any paintings.
                                     (D) He doesn't know what to do.

Sample Answer

You learn from the conversation that neither the man nor the woman likes the painting. The best answer to the question, "What does the man mean?" is (A), "He doesn't like the painting either." Therefore, the correct choice is (A).

1. (A) Tomorrow afternoon.
   (B) This morning.
   (C) Tomorrow morning.
   (D) In a few days.
   Ⓐ Ⓑ Ⓒ Ⓓ

2. (A) Turn on the lights.
   (B) Leave with the man.
   (C) Turn off the lights.
   (D) Leave before the man.
   Ⓐ Ⓑ Ⓒ Ⓓ

3. (A) The news.
   (B) A series.
   (C) A documentary.
   (D) A movie.
   Ⓐ Ⓑ Ⓒ Ⓓ

4. (A) The woman.
   (B) Mary.
   (C) John.
   (D) The man.
   Ⓐ Ⓑ Ⓒ Ⓓ

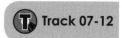
Directions: In this part, you will hear longer conversations. After each conversation, you will hear several questions. The conversations and questions will not be repeated.

After you hear a question, read the four possible answers in your test book and choose the best answer. Then, on your answer sheet, find the number of the question and fill in the space that corresponds to the letter of the answer you have chosen.

Remember, you are **NOT** allowed to take notes or write in your test book.

5. (A) Reporting test results.
(B) Preparing an examination.
(C) Publishing textbooks.
(D) Scheduling a meeting.
Ⓐ Ⓑ Ⓒ Ⓓ

6. (A) She is an instructor.
(B) She is an author.
(C) She is a publisher.
(D) She is a student.
Ⓐ Ⓑ Ⓒ Ⓓ

7. (A) Check questions.
(B) Print question booklets.
(C) Manage recordings.
(D) Arrange answer sheets.
Ⓐ Ⓑ Ⓒ Ⓓ

8. (A) Two thousand people will take the test.
(B) To allow for problems.
(C) The same number will be sold.
(D) So they can send out samples.
Ⓐ Ⓑ Ⓒ Ⓓ

Part C

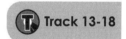

Directions: In this part, you will hear several talks. After each talk, you will hear some questions. The talks and questions will not be repeated. After you hear a question, read the four possible answers in your test book and choose the best answer. Then, on your answer sheet, find the number of the question and fill in the space that corresponds to the letter of the answer you have chosen.

Here is an example.
On the recording, you will hear:

Now listen to a sample question.
In your test book, you will read: (A) To demonstrate the latest use of computer graphics.   **Sample Answer**
(B) To discuss the possibility of an economic depression.   Ⓐ Ⓑ ● Ⓓ
(C) To explain the workings of the brain.
(D) To dramatize a famous mystery story.

The best answer to the question, "What is the main purpose of the program?" is (C), "To explain the workings of the brain." Therefore, the correct choice is (C).

Now listen to another sample question.

In your test book, you will read:　(A) It is required of all science majors.

Sample Answer

Ⓐ Ⓑ Ⓒ ●

(B) It will never be shown again.

(C) It can help viewers improve their memory skills.

(D) It will help with course work.

The best answer to the question, "Why does the speaker recommend watching the program?" is (D), "It will help with course work." Therefore, the correct choice is (D).

Remember, you are **NOT** allowed to take notes or write in your test book.

9. (A) That recently lower profits will slow it.
   (B) That groups are powerless to stop it.
   (C) That fish farming may solve it.
   (D) That environmentalists are unconcerned about it.

Ⓐ Ⓑ Ⓒ Ⓓ

10. (A) They can set legal limits on fishing for them.
    (B) They study about how to raise them.
    (C) They capture young ones for research.
    (D) They called for a ban on catching them.

Ⓐ Ⓑ Ⓒ Ⓓ

11. (A) The WWF.
    (B) The European Union.
    (C) The ICCAT.
    (D) Greenpeace.

Ⓐ Ⓑ Ⓒ Ⓓ

12. (A) It is higher than scientists recommended.
    (B) It is intended to stop tuna "ranching."
    (C) It is much lower than in past years.
    (D) It was lower than fishermen hoped.

Ⓐ Ⓑ Ⓒ Ⓓ

Section 2
Structure and Written Expression
Time: 7 minutes

This section is designed to measure your ability to recognize language that is appropriate for standard written English. There are two types of questions in this section, with special directions for each type.

(**Structure**)

Directions: Questions 1-5 are incomplete sentences. Beneath each sentence you will see four words or phrases, marked (A), (B), (C), and (D). Choose the one word or phrase that best completes the sentence. Then, on your answer sheet, find the number of the question and fill in the space that corresponds to the letter of the answer you have chosen. Fill in the space so that the letter inside the oval cannot be seen.

Example I

Geysers have often been compared to volcanoes ------- they both emit hot liquids from below the Earth's surface.

(A) due to   (C) in spite of

(B) because   (D) regardless of

Sample Answer

The sentence should read, "Geysers have often been compared to volcanoes because they both emit hot liquids from below the Earth's surface." Therefore, you should choose answer (B).

Example II

During the early period of ocean navigation, ------- any need for sophisticated instruments and techniques.

(A) so that hardly   (C) hardly was

(B) where there hardly was   (D) there was hardly

Sample Answer

The sentence should read, "During the early period of ocean navigation, there was hardly any need for sophisticated instruments and techniques." Therefore, you should choose answer (D).

Now begin work on the questions.

1. Pet therapy is a widely ------- form of psychological treatment.
   (A) accepted
   (B) acceptance
   (C) accepting
   (D) accepts

2. -------, the benefits of exercise outweigh the dangers.
   (A) The debate goes on
   (B) It has yet to be determined
   (C) For the most part
   (D) The reason it exists

3. Yesterday ------- much hotter if it hadn't been for the clouds.
   (A) was not that
   (B) would have been
   (C) was going to
   (D) had not been

4. A number ------- science experiments are aimed at discovering causes of cancer.
   (A) to
   (B) at
   (C) on
   (D) of

5. Government economists ------- guiding the national financial system.
   (A) find main causes of
   (B) have the right to
   (C) are mostly helpless
   (D) are responsible for

Written Expression

Directions: In questions 6-10 each sentence has four underlined words or phrases. The four underlined parts of the sentence are marked (A), (B), (C), and (D). Identify the one underlined word or phrase that must be changed in order for the sentence to be correct. Then, on your answer sheet, find the number of the question and fill in the space that corresponds to the letter of the answer you have chosen.

Example I

Guppies are sometimes <u>call</u> rainbow <u>fish</u> <u>because of</u> the males' <u>bright</u> colors.
                A   B   C   D

Sample Answer
● Ⓑ Ⓒ Ⓓ

The sentence should read, "Guppies are sometimes called rainbow fish because of the males' bright colors." Therefore, you should choose answer (A).

Example II

<u>Serving</u> several <u>term</u> in Congress, Shirley Chisholm became an <u>important</u>
  A   B   C
United States <u>politician</u>.
             D

Sample Answer
Ⓐ ● Ⓒ Ⓓ

The sentence should read, "Serving several terms in Congress, Shirley Chisholm became an important United States politician." Therefore, you should choose answer (B).

Now begin work on the questions.

---

6. Professor Franks <u>value</u> writing ability <u>more than</u> any <u>other</u> academic <u>skill</u>.
                         A   B   C   D   Ⓐ Ⓑ Ⓒ Ⓓ

7. Amy Barnes <u>is</u> the longest <u>service</u> state <u>senator</u> <u>in the</u> state of Ohio.
                  A   B   C   D   Ⓐ Ⓑ Ⓒ Ⓓ

8. When job hunting, remember <u>that a</u> first-class <u>resume</u> will catch <u>the eye</u> of any good <u>personal</u>
                                   A   B   C   D
director.
                                                             Ⓐ Ⓑ Ⓒ Ⓓ

9. You <u>can get</u> information about <u>enrolling</u> in advanced placement <u>course</u> in the <u>administration</u>
              A   B   C   D
building.
                                                             Ⓐ Ⓑ Ⓒ Ⓓ

10. The final examination will <u>covering</u> course <u>content</u> from the <u>entire</u> semester.
       A   B   C   D   Ⓐ Ⓑ Ⓒ Ⓓ

Section 3
Reading Comprehension
Time: 10 minutes

Directions: In this section you will read several passages. Each one is followed by several questions about it. For questions 1-10, you are to choose the one best answer, (A), (B), (C), or (D), to each question. Then, on your answer sheet, find the number of the question and fill in the space that corresponds to the letter of the answer you have chosen. Answer all questions following a passage on the basis of what is stated or implied in that passage.

Read the following passage:

> The railroad was not the first institution to impose regularity on society, or to draw attention to the importance of precise timekeeping. For as long as merchants have set out their wares at daybreak and communal festivities have been celebrated, people have been in rough agreement with their neighbors as to the time of day. The value of this tradition is today more apparent than ever. Were it not for public acceptance of a single yardstick of time, social life *5* would be unbearably chaotic: the massive daily transfers of goods, services, and information would proceed in fits and starts; the very fabric of modern society would begin to unravel.

Example I

What is the main idea of the passage?

(A) In modern society we must make more time for our neighbors.

(B) The traditions of society are timeless.

(C) An accepted way of measuring time is essential for the smooth functioning of society.

(D) Society judges people by the times at which they conduct certain activities.

Sample Answer

Ⓐ Ⓑ ● Ⓓ

The main idea of the passage is that societies need to agree about how time is to be measured in order to function smoothly. Therefore, you should choose answer (C).

Example II

In line 4, the phrase "this tradition" refers to

(A) the practice of starting the business day at dawn

(B) friendly relations between neighbors

(C) the railroad's reliance on time schedules

(D) people's agreement on the measurement of time

Sample Answer

Ⓐ Ⓑ Ⓒ ●

The phrase "this tradition" refers to the preceding clause, "people have been in rough agreement with their neighbors as to the time of day." Therefore, you should choose answer (D).

Now begin work on the questions.

Questions 1-10

The Gold Rush period of 1848 to 1855 influenced California more than any other era in its history. Before the precious mineral was discovered in January 1848 at the famous Sutter's Mill, the territory was quiet, under-populated, and little known to people around the world. After the Gold Rush, California had a substantially increased population, well-developed industries, and, of course, it was viewed as a place where new beginnings were sought and success could be found.

During the Gold Rush, some 300,000 people coming to the area to find fortune established settlements, which greatly increased the territory's population. For example, between 1847 and 1870, population increases in San Francisco expanded it from a small 500-person community to a relative metropolis of 150,000. This influx of new citizens occurred mainly in 1849, which is why the people of the Gold Rush are called 49ers. (It is interesting to note that a modern day San Francisco football team also has the same nostalgic name.)

To feed this larger population, California agriculture expanded to a grand scale that exists to this day. In addition, industrial mining techniques were needed leading to the advancement of manufacturing and marketing of new equipment. Furthermore, transportation industries such as railroads and hospitality businesses sprang up to meet the influx of the 49ers. By the mid-1850s, only big mining businesses could profit from gold mining itself, but the population and economy had grown large and diverse enough for citizens to make livings in many ordinary occupations.

As the Gold Rush helped define California in a substantial way, the new state became known as the birthplace of the "California Dream." Instead of being just a location, California was transformed into a state of mind where dreams could be fulfilled through new beginnings, hard work, and a little fortune. According to historian H. W. Brands, this "California Dream" spread to become the "American Dream" where success could be "won in a twinkling by audacity and good luck." One can only wonder what would have come of California and the "American Dream" if gold weren't discovered at old Sutter's Mill.

1. What is the main theme of this passage?
   (A) How a larger population extended the Gold Rush.
   (B) How an agriculture-based economy was developed.
   (C) How California became an independent territory.
   (D) How the discovery of gold transformed California.
   Ⓐ Ⓑ Ⓒ Ⓓ

2. What can be said of California before the Gold Rush?
   (A) It was controlled by Europe.
   (B) It was an isolated area.
   (C) It was a place people often visited.
   (D) It was economically developed.
   Ⓐ Ⓑ Ⓒ Ⓓ

3. The word "settlements" in line 8 is closest in meaning to
   (A) businesses
   (B) agreements
   (C) regulations
   (D) communities
   Ⓐ Ⓑ Ⓒ Ⓓ

4. According to the article, 300,000 people
   (A) worked in gold mines
   (B) moved from San Francisco
   (C) became California farmers
   (D) immigrated to California
   Ⓐ Ⓑ Ⓒ Ⓓ

5. When was gold discovered at Sutter's Mill?
   (A) 1847
   (B) 1849
   (C) 1848
   (D) 1850
   Ⓐ Ⓑ Ⓒ Ⓓ

6. The term "sprang up" in line 17 is closest in meaning to
   (A) relocated
   (B) purchased
   (C) emerged
   (D) secured
   Ⓐ Ⓑ Ⓒ Ⓓ

7. The word "occupations" in line 20 is closest in meaning to
   (A) towns
   (B) houses
   (C) mines
   (D) jobs
   Ⓐ Ⓑ Ⓒ Ⓓ

8. The third paragraph is mainly concerned with
   (A) the development of new industries
   (B) the effect of California on other states
   (C) the result of gold mining on nature
   (D) the redistribution of populations
   Ⓐ Ⓑ Ⓒ Ⓓ

9. The term "state of mind" in line 23 is closest in meaning to
   (A) belief
   (B) nation
   (C) county
   (D) discovery
   Ⓐ Ⓑ Ⓒ Ⓓ

10. What is historian H. W. Brands' opinion of the "California Dream"?
    (A) It was based on nothing but luck.
    (B) It influenced the entire nation.
    (C) It would have happened anywhere.
    (D) It was affected by other territories.
    Ⓐ Ⓑ Ⓒ Ⓓ

Unit
01
The Racial Discrimination Problem

Unit 1 は 1964 年に制定された米国の公民権法についてです。その中でも特に人を雇用する場合、性別、人種、肌の色などを理由に差別することを禁止している第7条について書かれたパッセージを読んでいきます。

Task 1 以下のパッセージを読みなさい。

Task 2 時間を意識して右の設問を解きなさい。理想は、設問ひとつにつき1分以内で解けることですが、今回は15分程度にタイマーを設定し、5問以上の正解を目指します。

※ Task は順に学習しても、p. 18 の Vocabulary Check! を先に行ってからでも構いません。

 **Track 02**

The Civil Rights Act of 1964 represents a landmark change in race relations of the United States of America. Although provisions for equal voter registration and ending racial segregation were included in the ultimate act, the element that affects issues of employment most is Title VII. While the original proposal was primarily constructed to protect African Americans, it was later modified to protect all minorities, white people, *5* and women as well.

In essence, Title VII of the Civil Rights Act of 1964 aims to protect citizens against employment discrimination based on gender, race, color, national origin, and religion. The title applies to organizations with fifteen or more employees, all federal, state, and local governments, employment agencies, and labor organizations as well. *10* Specifically, Title VII states that employment opportunities cannot be denied on an unequal basis to any individual due to his or her gender, racial group (or supposed racial group), race-linked physical characteristics, or even private association with someone of a particular race. Title VII also makes it unlawful to base employment decisions on stereotypes about abilities, traits, or the performance of individuals within *15* particular groups.

With specific regards to recruiting, hiring, and advancement, Title VII states that job requirements must be evenly and consistently applied to individuals of all genders, races, and colors. According to the title, a job requirement may not be applied evenly, for example, if: applications are gathered from a limited race or color-specific group; *20* workers are required to have backgrounds that are not work-specific; and testing is conducted with future or current employees for knowledge, skills, or abilities that are not work-related.

Although some thirty thousand charges are filed annually, Title VII of the Civil Rights Act of 1964 has gone far to resolve discrimination-based employment issues in *25* the United States of America.

Try the TOEFL Test!

Task TOEFL テストの Section 3 形式の問題です。左ページのパッセージに関する 10 の設問に挑戦しなさい。

1. The passage is mainly about the Civil Rights Act's
   (A) employment issues
   (B) voter registration matters
   (C) ban on segregation
   (D) equal education opportunities ⒶⒷⒸⒹ

2. The word "ultimate" in line 3 is closest in meaning to
   (A) major
   (B) timely
   (C) final
   (D) special ⒶⒷⒸⒹ

3. Which of the following constitutes a job requirement not being applied evenly?
   (A) Non work-related backgrounds are required of workers.
   (B) Testing of employees is conducted for work-related skills.
   (C) New worker applications are solicited from a variety of sources.
   (D) Employees are screened for abilities that help them work well. ⒶⒷⒸⒹ

4. The phrase "in essence" in line 7 is closest in meaning to
   (A) contradictorily
   (B) basically
   (C) additionally
   (D) oppositely ⒶⒷⒸⒹ

5. The author mentions all of the following as factors to which Title VII applies EXCEPT
   (A) sex
   (B) nationality
   (C) age
   (D) ethnicity ⒶⒷⒸⒹ

6. The word "traits" in line 15 is closest in meaning to
   (A) capabilities
   (B) applications
   (C) presentations
   (D) characteristics ⒶⒷⒸⒹ

7. What is the minimum number of employees an organization must have for Title VII to be applied?
   (A) 7
   (B) 19
   (C) 64
   (D) 15 ⒶⒷⒸⒹ

8. The word "advancement" in line 17 is closest in meaning to
   (A) advertisement
   (B) unfairness
   (C) promotion
   (D) dependability ⒶⒷⒸⒹ

9. According to the passage, thirty thousand employment discrimination charges are filed
   (A) monthly
   (B) yearly
   (C) hourly
   (D) daily ⒶⒷⒸⒹ

10. Where in the passage does the author provide a phrase for the national administration?
   (A) Line 1
   (B) Line 9
   (C) Line 19
   (D) Line 24 ⒶⒷⒸⒹ

Vocabulary Check!

Task 1 イラストを参考に、次の単語の意味を答えなさい。

1. gender   2. labor   3. race

_____   _____   _____

Task 2 次の単語と、それに対応する意味を線で結びなさい。

1. characteristics   •   • **a.** 人種差別、隔離
2. individual   •   • **b.** 少数派、少数民族
3. minority   •   • **c.** 特徴、持ち味
4. segregation   •   • **d.** 固定概念
5. stereotype   •   • **e.** 個人（の）

Task 3 次の単語と同様の意味を持つ語群を線で結びなさい。

1. represent   •   • **a.** change / alter / convert
2. include   •   • **b.** particular / characteristic / distinguishing
3. construct   •   • **c.** build / manufacture / create
4. modify   •   • **d.** stand for / symbolize
5. apply   •   • **e.** refuse / reject / contradict
6. specific   •   • **f.** encompass / contain
7. deny   •   • **g.** affect / relate / request
8. conduct   •   • **h.** record / register
9. charge   •   • **i.** handle / carry out / manage
10. file   •   • **j.** accusation / indictment
11. annually   •   • **k.** work out / answer / decipher
12. resolve   •   • **l.** once a year / per year / yearly

> **Tips**
> 同じ意味合いを持つ単語を一緒にまとめて覚えると、記憶に残りやすくなります。また同じ意味を持つ単語を答えさせる問題にも強くなります。

Building Reading Skills!

One Point Grammar

重要な接続詞

● 順接　and, so (that), therefore
　⇔　逆接　but, yet, although, though, while

● 重要な表現
　not only A but also B / as well as / neither A nor B / either A or B / whether A or not

Task 1 p. 16 のパッセージから抜粋した英文です。下線部に注意し、意味を正確に理解するようにしなさい。

<u>Although</u> provisions for equal voter registration and ending racial segregation were included in the ultimate act, the element that affects issues of employment most is Title VII. <u>While</u> the original proposal was primarily constructed to protect African Americans, it was later modified to protect all minorities, white people, and women as well.

Task 2 文意が通るように、括弧から適切な語句を選びなさい。

1. Salmon lay their eggs in fresh water **(although / because / and)** they live in salt water during most of their adult lives.

2. You might consider walking around town during your visit here. However, don't do this **(if / without / unless)** you have a very good sense of direction.

3. I heard that canned goods became more common **(while / during / when)** the 1860s, but supplies remained low. Why? Because, cans were made by hand in those days.

4. **(Either / Whether / Though)** you agree or not, I won't change my mind. I strongly believe that children should be taught mathematics at a very young age.

Task 3 A ～ D の下線部のうち、間違っている個所を指摘しなさい。また、その訂正方法も答えなさい。

1. While the original plan was mainly constructing to protect African Americans, it was
     A   B

   later revised to protect all minorities, white people, and women as well.
       C   D

   (   ) ⇒ _____

2. Railroads contributed to growth of the local industries because of by connecting major
               A   B

   city centers, but also by consuming enormous amounts of fuel.
                     C   D

   (   ) ⇒ _____

3. New employees will be requiring to take tests for knowledge, skills, or abilities that
                        A   B   C

   are work-related.
       D

   (   ) ⇒ _____

Try the TOEFL Test!

Task TOEFL テストの Section 2 形式の問題です。
Part A では空所に適切な語句を選び、Part B では A ～ D の下線部のうち間違っているものを選びなさい。

Part A: Structure

1. ------- their military role, forts provided numerous other benefits for people of the
   American West.
   (A) In addition to
   (B) Because of
   (C) Due to
   (D) In spite of

   Ⓐ Ⓑ Ⓒ Ⓓ

2. Unfortunately, melting ice has ------- around and find food.

    (A) a difficult situation for polar bears to move

    (B) made it difficult for polar bears to move

    (C) made polar bears to move

    (D) difficult problems for polar bears if they move

                                                                                            Ⓐ Ⓑ Ⓒ Ⓓ

Part B: Written Expression

1. Light waves <u>travel faster</u> than sound waves <u>do</u> <u>both</u> thunder and lightning are
                   A   **B** **C**

produced <u>at the same time</u>.
         D   Ⓐ Ⓑ Ⓒ Ⓓ

2. All dinosaurs <u>used to</u> be classified as cold-blooded reptiles, but recent evidence
                   A

while eating habits, posture, and skeletal structure <u>suggests</u> some may <u>have been</u>
 B   **C**   **D**

warm-blooded.
                                                                 Ⓐ Ⓑ Ⓒ Ⓓ

3. <u>While</u> walking around in the woods, you might be <u>tempted to</u> try some berries.
  A   **B**

<u>However</u>, you shouldn't eat them <u>unless you are not</u> certain about what they are.
  C   **D**   Ⓐ Ⓑ Ⓒ Ⓓ

4. <u>During</u> the birds choose <u>where to build</u> their nests, their choices are
  A   **B**

<u>based not only on</u> the branch itself but also on what <u>hangs over it</u>.
      C   **D**   Ⓐ Ⓑ Ⓒ Ⓓ

Unit 02

Short Conversations

Unit 2 では、大学やふだんの生活に関連した会話を聞きます。短い内容なので、あっという間に終わってしまいます。集中して聞くようにしましょう。

Try the TOEFL Test!

Task TOEFL テストの Section 1: Part A 形式の問題です。
短い会話を聞き、それぞれの内容に関する設問に答えなさい。

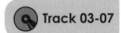 Track 03-07

1. (A) He has no idea about Jane's whereabouts.
   (B) He doesn't think the woman should see Jane.
   (C) Jane must return books to the library.
   (D) Jane might be in the library to study.

   Ⓐ Ⓑ Ⓒ Ⓓ

2. (A) He is too busy to meet her.
   (B) He is going to move tomorrow.
   (C) He wants the woman to come to his house.
   (D) He doesn't know what to do tomorrow.

   Ⓐ Ⓑ Ⓒ Ⓓ

3. (A) Call Amy to talk about a job.
   (B) Take a job in the library.
   (C) The man should take a bus to the museum.
   (D) There is not a single museum worth visiting.

   Ⓐ Ⓑ Ⓒ Ⓓ

4. (A) Mr. Nelson's lectures are easy.
   (B) She thinks it's boring.
   (C) She has a lot of homework to do.
   (D) It will be useful for her future.

   Ⓐ Ⓑ Ⓒ Ⓓ

5. (A) She will understand some poems.
   (B) The man should take extra classes.
   (C) She is available every Friday.
   (D) The man should help her with homework.

   Ⓐ Ⓑ Ⓒ Ⓓ

Building Listening Skills!

Task 左ページの５つの会話です。音声を聞き、下線部に入る語句を
書き取りなさい。

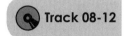
Track 08-12

1. A: Have you seen Jane today?
   B: Why don't you ①_____ the library?
      I ②_____ if she were sleeping there.
      She's been studying very hard.

2. A: Can you ③_____ some time for me tomorrow?
      I need some advice from you.
   B: ④_____ tomorrow. Do you know my address?

3. A: I'm just wondering if you know someone ⑤_____ having a
      part-time job at the library.
   B: I think Amy, a bookworm, might be.
      ⑥_____ and see if she would like to take the job.

4. A: Hi, how's the ⑦_____ you started this year?
   B: Well, I think ⑧_____ the assignments
      Mr. Nelson gives us every week.

5. A: Carla, can you help me ⑨_____ my notes?
      I can't ⑩_____ how to interpret some of these poems.
   B: I wish I could, but I'm ⑪_____ my ears in homework.
      I heard there are review sessions held every Friday that are really helpful.

Speaking

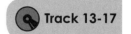
Task 1 p. 22 の英文のうち、重要な個所を抜粋しています。
まず、英文を見ながら、音声に合わせて、音読しなさい。

Task 2 ［ペア・ワーク］ペアになって、本当に会話をしているつもりで英文を言いなさい。必ず相手の目を見ながら行うこと。

Task 3 慣れてきたら右側の日本語だけを見て、英語をスラスラ読めるようになるまで練習しなさい。

English	Japanese
A: Have you seen Jane today? B: Why don't you try the library? I wouldn't be surprised if she were sleeping there. She's been studying very hard.	A: 今日ジェーンを見かけましたか。 B: 図書館を見てみたら？　彼女がそこで寝ていても不思議はないですよ。とても一生懸命勉強していますから。
A: Can you spare some time for me tomorrow? I need some advice from you. B: I'm off tomorrow. Do you know my address?	A: 明日時間がありますか。アドバイスをいただきたいのです。 B: 明日は休みです。私の住所を知っていますか。
A: I'm just wondering if you know someone interested in having a part-time job at the library. B: I think Amy, a bookworm, might be. I'll call her and see if she would like to take the job.	A: 誰か図書館でのアルバイトをしたい人をご存じですか。 B: 本の虫、エイミーがしたいかもしれません。電話をして、仕事をしたいか聞いてみますね。
A: Hi, how's the course you started this year? B: Well, I think I'm just getting used to the assignments Mr. Nelson gives us every week.	A: 今年始めたコースはどんな様子ですか。 B: そうですね、ネルソン教授が毎週出す宿題に、やっと慣れてきたかなというところです。
A: Carla, can you help me go over my notes? I can't figure out how to interpret some of these poems. B: I wish I could, but I'm up to my ears in homework. I heard there are review sessions held every Friday that are really helpful.	A: カーラ、ノートを復習するのを手伝ってもらえませんか。どのように解釈すればいいのかわからない詩がいくつかあるんです。 B: 手伝いたいのはやまやまだけど、私も自分の宿題に追われています。毎週金曜日にとても役立つ復習タイムがあるそうですよ。

Vocabulary Check!

Task 1 空所に入る適切な語句をそれぞれ下から選びなさい。

1. Everything needed for the meeting will be ready -------.
   - ☐ **a.** on time
   - ☐ **b.** by the time
   - ☐ **c.** at a time
   - ☐ **d.** for the time being

2. Could you tell me where to ------- the bus, please?
   - ☐ **a.** turn off
   - ☐ **b.** put off
   - ☐ **c.** get off
   - ☐ **d.** take off

3. Could you ------- some notebooks for me?
   - ☐ **a.** pick off
   - ☐ **b.** pick up
   - ☐ **c.** pick on
   - ☐ **d.** pick at

4. I had no time to ------- the grocery to buy some milk, sorry.
   - ☐ **a.** drop off
   - ☐ **b.** fill out
   - ☐ **c.** hold on
   - ☐ **d.** stop by

5. A calculator should really ------- handy in this class since we'll be doing a lot with statistics.
   - ☐ **a.** come by
   - ☐ **b.** come in
   - ☐ **c.** come down
   - ☐ **d.** come up

Task 2 A の発言に対する B の応答として適切なものを a ～ e から選びなさい。

1. A: Dr. Hill's lecture is great!   B: _____
2. A: What took you so long?   B: _____
3. A: Let's race to the top of the hill.   B: _____
4. A: Need a hand with the box?   B: _____
5. A: Got the time?   B: _____

a. I think I can manage.

b. You can say that again.

c. It's half past eight.

d. No thanks. I'm really out of shape.

e. My mother called me when I was about to leave.

One Point Grammar

One Point Grammar

名詞

次の3点に注意します。
特に「数えられない名詞」は基本的なことですが、しっかりおさらいしておくこと。

．．

1. 数えられない名詞に注意
   rain snow water music weather news information furniture
   equipment machinery scenery advice baggage [luggage] luck progress
   audience courage knowledge fun など

2. 常に複数形で用いる名詞
   species series means など

3. 単数形と複数形では意味が変わる名詞
   work—works room—rooms damage—damages respect—respects

Task 下線部が正しければ○、誤りを含む場合は、訂正方法を答えなさい。

1. What a great news!
   (   ) ⇒ _____

2. Could you give me some advice?
   (   ) ⇒ _____

3. Did you enjoy a good weather during your holiday?
   (   ) ⇒ _____

4. You have a lot of courage.
   (   ) ⇒ _____

5. Children should show respects to their parents.
   (   ) ⇒ _____

6. I guess even bad news are very welcome now.
   (   ) ⇒ _____

7. They still use those old machineries.
   (   ) ⇒ _____

8. Making friends is an important part of your school days.
   (   ) ⇒ _____

Try the TOEFL Test!

Task TOEFL テストの Section 2 形式の問題です。

Part A では空所に適切な語句を選び、Part B では A 〜 D の下線部のうち間違っているものを選びなさい。

Part A: Structure

1. As the drafter of this regulation set up the system, the management would,

   -------, choose hardworking and honest people as their employees.
   (A) how to display their own knowledge
   (B) otherwise their own knowledge
   (C) out of their own knowledge
   (D) for all their knowledge

   Ⓐ Ⓑ Ⓒ Ⓓ

2. Warm-blooded animals are usually active ------- because their body temperatures

   can adjust to the temperature of their environment.
   (A) for both weather of cold and hot
   (B) in both cold and hot weather
   (C) when the weather is cold or hot
   (D) while the weather is cold and hot

   Ⓐ Ⓑ Ⓒ Ⓓ

Part B: Written Expression

1. The earliest layers of sedimentary rock in the cave contain extensive remains of
                                            A   B

   animals, primitive tools, and two or more specie of ape-like hominids.
            C   D

   Ⓐ Ⓑ Ⓒ Ⓓ

2. A few decades ago, our forebears accomplished this type of work by mean of
                                    A   B

   high-speed of photography using equipment now available in any laboratory.
                              C   D

   Ⓐ Ⓑ Ⓒ Ⓓ

3. There have been some periods in history when extraordinary progress were made
                     A   B   C

   within a relatively short span of time.
          D

   Ⓐ Ⓑ Ⓒ Ⓓ

4. As technology has developed and knowledge of health-related aspects of various
                  A   B

   chemicals have increased, the list of environmental pollutants has lengthened.
            C   D

   Ⓐ Ⓑ Ⓒ Ⓓ

Unit 03

The Discovery of a New Medicine

Unit 3 のパッセージは、ある細菌の発見の歴史についてです。発見の過程と、それにまつわる驚くべきエピソードが紹介されています。

Task 1 以下のパッセージを読みなさい。

Task 2 時間を意識して右の設問を解きなさい。理想は、設問ひとつにつき 1 分以内で解けることですが、今回は 12 分程度にタイマーを設定し、5 問以上の正解を目指します。

   * Task は順に学習しても、p. 30 の Vocabulary Check! を先に行ってからでも構いません。

Track 18

The discovery of causes of diseases and development of medicines to treat them often happens in astonishing ways. One remarkable story is that of helicobacter pylori (H. pylori), a type of bacteria which has been found to cause serious stomach disorders. Two courageous scientists overcame erratic research and common assumptions about bacteria in the digestive system to find a remarkable cure to some terrible diseases.   5

Spiral-shaped bacteria were first noticed in the lining of a human stomach by German and Polish scientists in 1875 and 1899, but findings were inconclusive and underreported. A number of unconvincing studies were conducted in the first half of the 1900s, but interest unfortunately diminished after a 1954 study where American scientists failed to find stomach bacteria in over 1,000 stomach examinations.   10

When H. pylori was rediscovered in patients with stomach diseases in the 1970s, interest was renewed. Nobody was able to grow it, but in 1982, two Australian medical doctors, Barry Marshal and Robin Warren, tried to produce H. pylori. Their attempts were unsuccessful until they forgot to destroy the cultures before taking a five-day vacation. It magically turned out that five days was just the period needed for H. pylori   15 to grow.

However, because many doubted the bacteria's survival abilities in acidic stomach environments, their findings were met with great skepticism. To prove the bacteria's direct relationship with disease, Marshall amazingly drank a cocktail of H. pylori after which he became very ill. A subsequent examination showing the existence of both   20 H. pylori and gastric disease (which were absent before the experiment) in Marshall's stomach established proof of the bacteria's survival and effects. Antibiotics soon cured Marshall's suffering.

Thousands owe their thanks to these intrepid scientists who discovered the cause of a variety of dreadful illnesses. No wonder they won the Nobel Prize in 2005.   25

Try the TOEFL Test!

Task TOEFL テストの Section 3 形式の問題です。左ページのパッセージに関する 8 つの設問に挑戦しなさい。

1. The passage primarily discusses H. pylori's
   (A) verification
   (B) position
   (C) familiarity
   (D) treatment
   Ⓐ Ⓑ Ⓒ Ⓓ

2. According to the passage, H. pylori can be cultured in
   (A) three days
   (B) two days
   (C) five days
   (D) ten days
   Ⓐ Ⓑ Ⓒ Ⓓ

3. The word "erratic" in line 4 is closest in meaning to
   (A) excellent
   (B) inconsistent
   (C) difficult
   (D) competitive
   Ⓐ Ⓑ Ⓒ Ⓓ

4. The word "skepticism" in line 18 is closest in meaning to
   (A) popularity
   (B) honor
   (C) expense
   (D) disbelief
   Ⓐ Ⓑ Ⓒ Ⓓ

5. When did scientists fail to discover H. pylori in several stomachs?
   (A) 1982
   (B) 1970s
   (C) 1899
   (D) 1954
   Ⓐ Ⓑ Ⓒ Ⓓ

6. Which of the following is the main reason Barry Marshall drank H. pylori?
   (A) To show that it is harmless bacteria
   (B) To prove that it causes disease
   (C) To discover its incubation period
   (D) To promote a new medicine
   Ⓐ Ⓑ Ⓒ Ⓓ

7. The word "subsequent" in line 20 is closest in meaning to
   (A) following
   (B) thorough
   (C) failed
   (D) certain
   Ⓐ Ⓑ Ⓒ Ⓓ

8. The author suggests all of the following about H. pylori EXCEPT that
   (A) it is difficult to grow in a lab
   (B) it has been studied a long time
   (C) it can be killed with acid
   (D) it can survive in human stomachs
   Ⓐ Ⓑ Ⓒ Ⓓ

Vocabulary Check!

Task 1 次の語句と、それに対応する意味を線で結びなさい。

1. stomach disorders   •   • **a.** らせん状細菌
2. digestive system   •   • **b.** 胃の病気
3. terrible diseases   •   • **c.** 消化器系
4. spiral-shaped bacteria   •   • **d.** ひどい病気

Task 2 次のイメージを持つ単語を p. 28 のパッセージから探しなさい。ひとつとは限りません。

1.「素晴らしい」イメージ

_____

2.「ひどい・悪い」イメージ

_____

3.「病気」のイメージ

_____

4.「研究」のイメージ

_____

5.「勇気」のイメージ

_____

Task 3 in- / un- / re- などの接頭辞がついている単語を p. 28 のパッセージから探しなさい。
ひとつとは限りません。

_____   _____

_____   _____

_____   _____

_____

_____

_____

_____

Tips 単語ひとつだけで覚えるのではなく、remarkable cures（素晴らしい治療法）のように2語以上の句で覚えると忘れにくくなります。

Building Reading Skills!

One Point Grammar

仮定法

仮定法は次のように整理すると理解しやすい。

. . . .

1. 「もし〜なら、…かもしれない」と想像する場合、ふたつのパターンで表現できる。
   ① 〈If ＋主語＋動詞の原形 , 主語＋ will ＋動詞の原形〉

   If you **talk** to her, she **will understand** the situation.
   ② 〈If ＋主語＋過去形 , 主語＋ would ［could / should など］＋動詞の原形〉

   If you **talked** to her, she **would understand** the situation.
   ※①②ともに、現在や未来のことに対する仮定だが、②のほうはあまり実現性や可能性を考えていない。

2. 過去のことに対して、「もし（あの時）〜だったら、…だったかもしれない」と
   想像する場合
   〈If ＋主語＋ had ＋過去分詞 , 主語＋ would have ＋過去分詞〉

   If you **had talked** to her, she **would have understood** the situation.

Task 1 文意が通るように、括弧から適切な語句を選びなさい。

1. If Mars **(has / have / had)** air on it, we could live there without a spacesuit.
2. If I **(am / was / were)** you, I would decline such an offer.
3. I **(won't fail / wouldn't fail / wouldn't have failed)** that test if I had studied much harder.
4. **(If / Had / With)** it not been for the water, no one could have survived there.
5. **(Unless / Without / When)** transportation-related inventions such as steam locomotives
   and railroads, the pace of industrial development would have been slowed immeasurably.

Task 2 A ～ D の下線部のうち、間違っている個所を指摘しなさい。また、その訂正方法も答えなさい。

1. If Brooklyn <u>is</u> not a borough of New York City, it <u>would be</u> the fifth <u>largest</u> city <u>in</u> the
   　　　　　　 A 　　　　　　　　　　　　　　　　　　　　 B 　　　　　　 C 　　　　 D
   United States.

   (　　　) ⇒ ＿＿＿＿＿＿＿＿＿＿＿＿＿＿

2. <u>If</u> human beings <u>were</u> immortal, we <u>would</u> not <u>had to worry</u> about growing old.
   　A 　　　　　　 B 　　　　　　　　　 C 　　　　 D

   (　　　) ⇒ ＿＿＿＿＿＿＿＿＿＿＿＿＿＿

3. <u>If had</u> Mike not <u>been sick</u>, he <u>could</u> <u>have attended</u> the academic conference.
   　A 　　　　　　 B 　　　　 C 　　　 D

   (　　　) ⇒ ＿＿＿＿＿＿＿＿＿＿＿＿＿＿

4. The school counselor listed several things <u>that</u> the student <u>hadn't done</u> but <u>would have do</u>
   　　　　　　　　　　　　　　　　　　　　　　 A 　　　　　　　　　 B 　　　　　 C
   if he <u>had been</u> serious about his studies.
   　　　　 D

   (　　　) ⇒ ＿＿＿＿＿＿＿＿＿＿＿＿＿＿

Try the TOEFL Test!

Task TOEFL テストの Section 2 形式の問題です。
Part A では空所に適切な語句を選び、Part B では A ～ D の下線部のうち間違っているものを選びなさい。

Part A: Structure

1. The changes from the Old Stone Age to the New Stone Age never could have
   happened ------- the development of metal casting.
   (A) without
   (B) with
   (C) for
   (D) around

   Ⓐ Ⓑ Ⓒ Ⓓ

2. ------- some 65 million years ago, they would have continued to evolve into increasingly intelligent forms.

(A) Unless the dinosaurs become extinct

(B) The dinosaurs are not extinct

(C) If the dinosaurs not been extinct

(D) Had the dinosaurs not become extinct

Ⓐ Ⓑ Ⓒ Ⓓ

Part B: Written Expression

1. If there were not mitochondria in our cells, we could not have moved our muscles.
   A   B   C   D

Ⓐ Ⓑ Ⓒ Ⓓ

2. If the Earth's average temperature rose by only five degrees Celsius, human habitats
    A   B   C

undergo catastrophic changes.
  D

Ⓐ Ⓑ Ⓒ Ⓓ

3. If the smallpox virus, which only exists in laboratories these days, were released
     A   B   C

accidentally, people will be seriously hurt.
             D

Ⓐ Ⓑ Ⓒ Ⓓ

4. Human beings, plants, and animals have a "biological clock" which refers to
                                  A   B

the biological and chemical changes that occur with aging, as if a clock
                                     C

had been ticking away inside the body.
   D

Ⓐ Ⓑ Ⓒ Ⓓ

Looking for Reference Books in the Library

Unit 4 では、図書館での学生と司書の会話を題材に学習します。学生が尋ねている内容と、司書の返答に注意して音声を聞きましょう。

Try the TOEFL Test!

Task TOEFL テストの Section 1: Part B 形式の問題です。
長めの会話文を聞き、その内容に関する 4 つの設問に答えなさい。

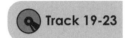 **Track 19-23**

1. (A) At a publishing company.
   (B) In a bookstore.
   (C) In a library.
   (D) At a business office.

   Ⓐ Ⓑ Ⓒ Ⓓ

2. (A) Work in the shelves section.
   (B) Work with the computer system.
   (C) Work on the first floor.
   (D) Work as a reference librarian.

   Ⓐ Ⓑ Ⓒ Ⓓ

3. (A) He met the woman at the wrong time.
   (B) He went to the wrong company.
   (C) He went to the wrong floor.
   (D) He wrote down the wrong number.

   Ⓐ Ⓑ Ⓒ Ⓓ

4. (A) She is sorry she couldn't help him more.
   (B) She didn't mind taking the time.
   (C) She regrets that it took so long.
   (D) She's happy he could find the fourth floor.

   Ⓐ Ⓑ Ⓒ Ⓓ

Building Listening Skills!

Task ▶ 左ページの会話文です。
音声を聞き、下線部に入る語句を書き取りなさい。

 Track 19

A: Excuse me. I hope I'm not ①_____, but I wonder if
you can help me ②_____ I'd like to borrow.

B: I usually just work here in the shelves. If you want to find ③_____
_____, you should use our computer system or talk to the
④_____ on the first floor.

A: I ⑤_____. I got the number, but I can't find the book anywhere.

B: OK. I might be able to help you find it. ⑥_____ the reference number?

A: Sure. ⑦_____. Sorry, but my writing is a little messy.

B: Yeah, I see ⑧_____. I can't understand what you wrote. Can you read it to me?

A: OK. It's KPW29913. I looked in the K section, but ⑨_____
_____ with that number.

B: Let's see that number again. Oh, I see. I thought ⑩_____
_____ with it.

A: ⑪_____ I thought I got the right number from the computer.

B: Book numbers always ⑫_____. The reference number you wrote ends
in a number.

A: Oops. Oh, I got it. It looks like I wrote thirteen ⑬_____ a B at the end.
The real number should have a B instead of thirteen.

B: ⑭_____. It should be over here. Yes, here it is.

A: Oh, thanks a lot for your help. Sorry ⑮_____ for so long.

B: That's OK. ⑯_____ anyway.

unit 4   35

Speaking

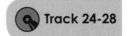

Task 1 p. 34 の会話文のうち、重要な個所を抜粋しています。

まず、英文を見ながら、音声に合せて、音読しなさい。

Task 2 [ペア・ワーク] ペアになって、ほんとうに会話しているつもりで、英文を言いなさい。必ず相手の目を見ながら行うこと。

Task 3 慣れてきたら右側の日本語だけを見て、英語でスラスラ言えるようになるまで練習しなさい。

English	Japanese
A: Excuse me. I wonder if you can help me find a book I'd like to borrow. B: If you want to find the location of a book, you should use our computer system or talk to the reference librarian on the first floor.	A: すみません。借りたい本を探すのを手伝っていただけるでしょうか。 B: 本がどこにあるかを見つけたいのなら、コンピュータ・システムを使うか、1階にいるリファレンス担当司書に相談してください。
B: Can you tell me the reference number? A: Sure. Here it is.	B: 照会番号を教えてください。 A: はい。これです。
A: Sorry, but my writing is a little messy. B: I see what you mean. I can't understand what you wrote.	A: すみません。字が少し雑で。 B: おっしゃることはわかります（＝そうですね）。なんと書いてあるのか、理解できません。
A: What's the problem? B: Book numbers always end in a letter. The reference number you wrote ends in a number.	A: 何が問題なのでしょうか。 B: 本の番号はいつも文字で終わるのです。あなたが書いた照会番号は数字で終わっています。
B: That makes more sense. It should be over here. Yes, here it is. A: Thanks a lot for your help.	B: それなら、もっとよくわかります。ここらへんにあるはずです。はいどうぞ。 A: 手伝ってくださってどうもありがとう。

Vocabulary Check!

Task 1 次の単語と、それに対応する意味を線で結びなさい。

1. date of issue   •
2. circulation   •
3. overdue book   •
4. revolving bookstand   •
5. procedure for checking out   •

  • **a.** 貸出部数
  • **b.** 回転書架
  • **c.** 貸出手順
  • **d.** 延滞図書
  • **e.** 貸出日

Task 2 次の単語と、その定義文、もしくは同様の意味を持つ語群を線で結びなさい。

1. register   •
2. faculty   •
3. permit   •
4. estate   •
5. contract   •
6. converse   •
7. evaluate   •
8. regulation   •
9. oversee   •
10. submit   •
11. availability   •

  • **a.** possession / property
  • **b.** a legal written agreement
  • **c.** record / enroll
  • **d.** estimate / rate / appraise
  • **e.** teaching staff / natural ability
  • **f.** supervise / manage / lead
  • **g.** propose / put forward / present
  • **h.** allow / assent / make something possible
  • **i.** contrary / opposite / speak (v)
  • **j.** possibility / status of booking / usability
  • **k.** official rules or orders

Tips

Section 1: Part B で使われることが多い単語を取り上げ、右側には、類語のみならず、単語の定義も示しました。英英辞書の定義に少しずつでも慣れておけば、より素早く単語を覚えられるようになるでしょう。

One Point Grammar

One Point Grammar

助動詞

助動詞で注意したいのは次の5点です。

....

1. **can**
   「〜できる」（能力）だけではなく、「〜であり得る」（可能性）の意味もある。
   Such a thing **can** happen. / It **can't** be true.

2. **may**
   「〜してもよい」と「〜かもしれない」の意味がある。
   May I go with you? / He **may** come late.

3. **must**
   「〜しなければならない」と「〜に違いない」の意味がある。
   You **must** finish it immediately. / Her story **must** be true.

4. **used to** の使い分け
   I **used to** work overnight. / I am **used to** working overnight.

5. 〈助動詞＋完了形〉の用法
   She **may have been** sick. / She **must have been** sick.
   She **can't have been** sick. / I **should have told** you so earlier.

(Task) 文意が通るように、括弧から適切な語句を選びなさい。

1. New water resources (**must / must be / can**) found for this community.
2. This committee (**should / used to / was used to**) meet to create a new dress code
   by the end of the month.
3. Information like this (**has not / cannot / can have**) be really useful unless it's made
   widely available.
4. Students (**had not better / had better not**) visit such a place.
5. You will write us, (**shan't / won't / can't**) you?
6. I (**must / had to / ought to**) attend the seminar last year.

Try the TOEFL Test!

Task TOEFL テストの Section 2 形式の問題です。

Part A では空所に適切な語句を選び、Part B では A ～ D の下線部のうち間違っているものを選びなさい。

Part A: Structure

1. To qualify for the program, students need to ------- in high school as well
   as receiving high test scores.
   (A) performed well
   (B) be performed well
   (C) being performed well
   (D) have performed well   Ⓐ Ⓑ Ⓒ Ⓓ

2. Some educators say that the goal of teaching is to help students learn what -------
   know to lead a happy and successful life.
   (A) they need to
   (B) do they need
   (C) may be needed for
   (D) to be needed for   Ⓐ Ⓑ Ⓒ Ⓓ

Part B: Written Expression

1. In order to <u>apply for</u> the position, this form <u>must be</u> filled out and <u>turn</u> in.
   A   B   C   D   Ⓐ Ⓑ Ⓒ Ⓓ

2. It <u>can be</u> inferred from her <u>ignorance</u> of bus schedules and locations that the
       A   B

   woman <u>is</u> not used to <u>take</u> the university shuttle bus.
          C   D   Ⓐ Ⓑ Ⓒ Ⓓ

3. The government <u>decided</u> that taxpayers ought <u>to not</u> fund research <u>for</u> other
                 A   B   C

   <u>nations</u>.
     D   Ⓐ Ⓑ Ⓒ Ⓓ

4. This chemical substance <u>must</u> have been discovered and <u>understand</u> as
                        A   B

   <u>a distinct</u> material <u>over</u> one thousand years ago.
     C   D   Ⓐ Ⓑ Ⓒ Ⓓ

The American Insurance System

Unit 5 では米国の保険制度について書かれたパッセージを読んでいきます。どのような保険の種類があるのか、制度の問題点は何なのかについて注意しながら読んでいきましょう。

Task 1 以下のパッセージを読みなさい。

Task 2 時間を意識して右の設問を解きなさい。理想は、設問ひとつにつき 1 分以内で解けることですが、今回は 10 分程度にタイマーを設定し、5 問以上の正解を目指します。

 ＊ Task は順に学習しても、p. 42 の Vocabulary Check! を先に行ってからでも構いません。

Track 29

　　The healthcare system in the United States of America is a very controversial one. Some of its aspects such as effectiveness and innovation get rather high ratings, while others such as cost and the general health of citizens receive less favorable ratings. Also, the U.S. has higher survival rates for certain cancers than other developed countries, yet still has the highest infant mortality rate. Some blame these ⁵ contradictions on the unequal distribution of health insurance among the insured and the uninsured.

　　Currently, around 85% of Americans (250 million) have some form of private health insurance and about 60% of those people (150 million) are insured by employers under group plans. In these cases, the employer usually carries much of the cost and ¹⁰ employees make up the rest. Additionally, either through an employer or by themselves, about 10% (25 million) of the insured population purchases individual (non-group) insurance where policyholders pay monthly fees and part of the total cost of treatment.

　　Of the 85% of insured Americans, around 30% of them (75 million)——including the elderly, disabled, children, veterans, and some of the poor——are covered under ¹⁵ public insurance plans. Examples of federally funded insurance plans include Medicare for citizens 65 and older, Medicaid for low income people, and the Veterans Administration, which provides healthcare to veterans.

　　Sadly, some Americans are not covered by employer plans or government-funded plans, and cannot afford private health insurance. In recent years, 15% of the American ²⁰ public (45 million) went uninsured for at least part of the year, and many of these people unfortunately did not get healthcare they urgently needed.

　　The paradox of people with access to health insurance getting the best healthcare and those without access to insurance getting less or none is perhaps the reason for so much political controversy at the national level over the years. Attempts to create ²⁵ a comprehensive national healthcare system have been made, but they have all failed. However valiant the efforts, it seems a shame that such a wealthy nation at the cutting edge of medical technology leaves 15% of its people without proper healthcare.

Try the TOEFL Test!

Task TOEFL テストの Section 3 形式の問題です。左ページのパッセージに関する 8 つの設問に挑戦しなさい。

1. What is the main theme of the passage?
   (A) Unequal access to healthcare
   (B) Differences between insurance plans
   (C) Innovations in healthcare
   (D) How to create a national healthcare plan
   Ⓐ Ⓑ Ⓒ Ⓓ

2. In the first paragraph, the author contrasts healthcare innovation with
   (A) efficiency
   (B) expense
   (C) treatment
   (D) cancer rates
   Ⓐ Ⓑ Ⓒ Ⓓ

3. The word "contradictions" in line 6 is closest in meaning to
   (A) advantages
   (B) comparisons
   (C) inconsistencies
   (D) similarities
   Ⓐ Ⓑ Ⓒ Ⓓ

4. According to the passage, 25 million Americans are
   (A) insured privately
   (B) uninsured
   (C) insured publicly
   (D) insured as a group
   Ⓐ Ⓑ Ⓒ Ⓓ

5. The word "veterans" in line 17 is closest in meaning to
   (A) elderly
   (B) disabled
   (C) politicians
   (D) soldiers
   Ⓐ Ⓑ Ⓒ Ⓓ

6. The word "urgently" in line 22 is closest in meaning to
   (A) expensively
   (B) optionally
   (C) importantly
   (D) thoughtlessly
   Ⓐ Ⓑ Ⓒ Ⓓ

7. Which statement best reflects the fourth paragraph's point about uninsured people?
   (A) They should buy insurance.
   (B) They still received healthcare.
   (C) The number will increase.
   (D) There are too many.
   Ⓐ Ⓑ Ⓒ Ⓓ

8. What does the author suggest is needed?
   (A) A reduction in prices for public healthcare
   (B) An all-inclusive national healthcare system
   (C) Better funding for medical research
   (D) Expanded membership in private insurance systems
   Ⓐ Ⓑ Ⓒ Ⓓ

Vocabulary Check!

Task 1 日本語の意味に合う単語（副詞）を、p. 40 のパッセージから探して書きなさい。

1. 現時点では （**c**　　　　　） = at the present time
2. 加えて　　（**a**　　　　　） = in addition
3. 不運にも　（**u**　　　　　） = unluckily
4. 緊急に　　（**u**　　　　　） = as soon as possible / immediately

Task 2 次の英文をよく読み、下線部の単語の意味を右側から選び、線で結びなさい。

In setting up the prices of life <u>insurance</u>, future <u>mortality</u> and <u>policyholder</u> behavior are key factors. Insurance companies carefully decide the balance of <u>fees</u> and <u>distribution</u> of funds.

1. insurance　　　•
2. mortality　　　•
3. policyholder　　•
4. fees　　　　　•
5. distribution　　•

- **a.** money regularly paid
- **b.** the number of deaths within a particular society and within a particular period of time
- **c.** the action of sharing something out among a number of recipients
- **d.** someone who has bought insurance for something
- **e.** an agreement in which you pay a company money and they pay your costs if you have an accident, injury, etc.

Task 3 次の単語と、その定義文、もしくは同様の意味を持つ語群を線で結びなさい。

1. controversial　　•
2. innovation　　　•
3. favorable　　　•
4. aspect　　　　•
5. blame　　　　　•
6. contradiction　•
7. attempt　　　　•
8. infant　　　　　•
9. comprehensive　•
10. valiant　　　　•

- **a.** originality / newness / inventiveness
- **b.** opposition / disagreement
- **c.** arguing / discrepant / clashing
- **d.** baby / beginning
- **e.** including everything / inclusive
- **f.** beneficial / promising / auspicious
- **g.** try / effort / endeavor
- **h.** part of situations, ideas, etc. / appearance
- **i.** courageous / very brave in a difficult situation
- **j.** find fault / condemn

Tips

単語をまず英英辞書で調べるだけでも、語彙力が伸びます。あとから英和の辞書で確認しても構いませんので、英英辞書に慣れましょう。定義を音読してスラスラ言えるようになれば、表現力や会話力も伸びます。

Building Reading Skills!

One Point Grammar

比較

比較で重要なのは次の３点です。

. . . .

1. 「A は B よりも〜」
   単語に er をつけて変化させるか、単語の前に more をつける。
   He is **taller than** I am.
   Pamela can sing **more beautifully than** Marco does.

2. 「A は（〜の中で）もっとも〜だ」
   単語に est をつけて変化させるか、単語の前に the most をつける。
   This is **the highest** mountain in my country.
   The 1920s was one of **the most** important periods for blues music.

3. 「A は B と同じくらい〜だ」
   as 〜 as を使う。
   He is **as** tall **as** I am.
   I want it **as** much **as** you do.

Task 1 p. 40 のパッセージから抜粋した英文です。下線部に注意し、意味を正確に理解するようにしなさい。

The U.S. has <u>higher</u> survival rates for certain cancers <u>than</u> other developed countries, yet still has <u>the highest</u> infant mortality rate. Some blame these contradictions on the unequal distribution of health insurance among the insured and the uninsured.

Task 2 文意が通るように、括弧から適切な語句を選びなさい。

1. Pluto is much **(small / smaller / more small)** than any other planet in the solar system and now classified as a "dwarf planet."

2. The **(cold / colder / coldest)** air temperature ever recorded on Earth is −89.2 °C (−129 °F), at Vostok Station, Antarctica.

3. Fats allow us to store energy, a far **(efficient / more efficient / the efficient)** energy source than having to constantly eat either carbohydrates or proteins.

4. The advent of "talkies" made the movie industry by far the **(popular / more popular / most popular)** form of entertainment during the 1930s.

5. The lunar calendar is synchronized to the lunar month rather **(or / than / ever)** the solar year.

6. Diesel engines are set to return to the U.S. because they don't burn much fuel and therefore emit **(more / less / clean)** carbon dioxide than gasoline engines do.

Task 3 A ～ D の下線部のうち、間違っている個所を指摘しなさい。また、その訂正方法も答えなさい。

1. One of <u>the most</u> important aspects of the Iron Age <u>are</u> that it <u>brought</u> highly effective
     　　　A 　　　　　　　　　　　　　　　　　　　B 　　　　　C

   weapons and agricultural tools to <u>large</u> populations.
   　　　　　　　　　　　　　　　　　　D

   (　　　　　) ⇒_____

2. <u>When</u> clouds reach a saturation point, <u>or</u> the point at which they can <u>no longest</u> contain
     A 　　　　　　　　　　　　　　　　　B 　　　　　　　　　　　　　　　　C

   their moisture, droplets <u>fall</u> to earth as rain or snow.
   　　　　　　　　　　　　D

   (　　　　　) ⇒_____

3. The method by which mosaics are made <u>hasn't</u> changed much since ancient times.
   　　　　　　　　　　　　　　　　　　　A

   The mosaic is one of the <u>most oldest</u> and <u>most durable</u> <u>forms</u> of artistic decoration.
   　　　　　　　　　　　　　　B 　　　　　　　C 　　　　　D

   (　　　　　) ⇒_____

Try the TOEFL Test!

Task ▶ TOEFL テストの Section 2 形式の問題です。
Part A では空所に適切な語句を選び、Part B では A ～ D の下線部のうち間違っているものを選びなさい。

Part A: Structure

1. A solar eclipse occurs when the moon moves in front of the Sun and hides ------- part of the Sun from Earth.
   (A) at most
   (B) at least
   (C) no more
   (D) no less

   Ⓐ Ⓑ Ⓒ Ⓓ

2. In mammals, ------- the brain is in proportion to total body weight, the greater the intelligence of the animal.
   (A) the larger
   (B) larger
   (C) largest
   (D) the large

   Ⓐ Ⓑ Ⓒ Ⓓ

Part B: Written Expression

1. The automobile <u>was</u> <u>far</u> the most significant economic and social <u>development</u>
             A   B   C

   of the <u>early</u> twentieth century.
        D

   Ⓐ Ⓑ Ⓒ Ⓓ

2. Surprisingly, Tyrannosaurus <u>was</u> a far <u>sleeker animal</u> previously thought, perhaps
                      A   B

   weighing <u>less than</u> 6 1/2 tons, <u>no more than</u> an elephant.
          C   D

   Ⓐ Ⓑ Ⓒ Ⓓ

3. The <u>so-called</u> American whitewood <u>is</u> one of <u>the most</u> valuable timber <u>product</u> in
        A   B   C   D

   the United States.

   Ⓐ Ⓑ Ⓒ Ⓓ

4. Experiments have shown that fish raised in a group <u>are</u> <u>best</u> at <u>avoiding</u> enemies
                                                 A B   C

   <u>in case of</u> actual danger than fish raised alone.
      D

   Ⓐ Ⓑ Ⓒ Ⓓ

Instructions on Class by a Professor

Unit 6 では、大学教授による授業のオリエンテーションを題材に学習します。特に、授業内容、成績のつけ方に注意して聞き取りを行いましょう。

Try the TOEFL Test!

Task TOEFL テストの Section 1: Part C 形式の問題です。
長めの英文を聞き、その内容に関する 4 つの設問に答えなさい。

Track 30-34

1. (A) Guest speakers.
   (B) World War II.
   (C) Course guidelines.
   (D) Test results.

   Ⓐ Ⓑ Ⓒ Ⓓ

2. (A) To hear important information.
   (B) Because homework assignments are given.
   (C) So they can receive materials.
   (D) In order to get attendance points.

   Ⓐ Ⓑ Ⓒ Ⓓ

3. (A) 12.
   (B) 15.
   (C) 30.
   (D) 10.

   Ⓐ Ⓑ Ⓒ Ⓓ

4. (A) International economics.
   (B) European culture.
   (C) Nineteenth century politics.
   (D) American history.

   Ⓐ Ⓑ Ⓒ Ⓓ

Building Listening Skills!

Task 1 左ページの英文音声を聞き、次の質問に答えなさい。できるだけ英語で答えること。

Q1. What are you going to study in this class?

_____

Q2. Will the professor call the roll?

_____

Q3. What kind of questions will be asked in the tests?

_____

Task 2 左ページの英文です。音声を聞き、下線部に入る語句を聞き取りなさい。

Good afternoon and welcome to History 202. ① _____ American politics, culture, and economics from the end of World War II ② _____. I hope you are all in the right classroom, interested in this topic, and ③ _____. First, I'll tell you the class rules, then I'll ④ _____ to give you a brief overview of the course contents.

Although I ⑤ _____ during the course, I strongly recommend that you attend all fifteen lectures. Some students choose to stay home and study ⑥ _____, but I'll give you lots of information that you can't find in books and it will ⑦ _____ appear on a test in one form or another.

I will give you ⑧ _____, but because students sometimes have bad days, I'll only ⑨ _____ in your final grade. There'll be some multiple-choice questions and one written one on each quiz and they ⑩ _____ percent of your final score. There'll also be ⑪ _____ worth 30 percent of your ending grade and a final examination that has multiple-choice and essay questions that's worth 40 percent.

If there aren't any questions, I'll continue ⑫ _____.

Speaking

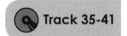

Task 1 p. 46 の英文のうち、重要な個所を抜粋しています。

まず、英文を見ながら、音声に合せて、音読しなさい。

Task 2 [ペア・ワーク] ペアになって、速く正確に読む競争をしなさい。1回目は同時にスタートし、2回目は負けた人が先にスタートし、2文目の in this course まで来たら、勝った人が追いかけなさい。

Task 3 慣れてきたら右側の日本語だけを見て、英文をスラスラ読めるようになるまで練習しなさい。

English	Japanese
Good afternoon and welcome to my American History class.	こんにちは、そして、私のアメリカ史の授業へようこそ。
I hope you are all interested in this course and ready to study hard.	皆さん全員がこのコースに関心を持ち、一生懸命勉強する気になっているといいのですが。
I'll give you a brief overview of the course contents.	コースの内容について簡潔に概要を説明します。
Although I won't check attendance during the course, I strongly recommend that you attend all lectures.	期間中出席は取りませんが、全講義に出席することを強く薦めます。
I'll give you lots of information that you can't find in books and it will most likely appear on tests.	本には載っていない情報をたくさんお伝えしますし、そこがテストにもよく出ます。
I will give you twelve short quizzes, a mid-term essay test, and a final examination.	小テストを12回、中間小論文、期末試験も実施します。
If there aren't any questions, I'll continue with the course overview.	何も質問がなければ、コース概要説明を続けます。

Vocabulary Check!

Task 1 下線部に入る適切な単語を語群から選び、書き写しなさい。

recommend	include	continue	attend	choosing	appear

1. I don't know much about this town. Could you _____ some good restaurants?
2. Are you going to _____ the seminar tomorrow? If so, would you get the handouts for me?
3. Do you have travel package tours that _____ some optional sightseeing?
4. Is there anything you do regularly like exercise or hobbies that you want to _____?
5. Do you think solar powered laptop computers will _____ in the market soon?
6. A growing number of young people today are _____ not to marry.

Task 2 p. 47 のスクリプトから、次の意味を持つ単語を探し出し、書き写しなさい。

1. 内容 _____ 2. 出席（の回数） _____

3. 点数 _____ 4. 小論文 _____

5. テスト _____ _____ _____

Task 3 次の語句と、それに対応する定義を線で結びなさい。

1. instruction • • a. a summarized description
2. lecture • • b. continuing for a short time
3. brief • • c. questions with several optional choices
4. overview • • d. information or statements telling you what to do
5. multiple-choice questions • • e. an educational talk given to a group of people

Tips 必ず発音しながら覚えるようにしていますか。書けることも大切ですが、まずは発音できるようにしましょう。

One Point Grammar

One Point Grammar

副詞

副詞で重要なのは次の3点です。

1. 副詞は動詞・形容詞・副詞を修飾し、名詞を修飾する形容詞と区別すること。
   Mike sings **well**. ------- 副詞
   Mike is a **good** singer. ------- 形容詞

2. 副詞は形容詞に ly をつけた形のものが多い。
   The family lived **happily**. ------- 副詞
   The family lived a **happy** life. ------- 形容詞

3. 形容詞にしなくてはいけない補語
   My mother looked **angry**. ------- この意味で副詞 angrily は使えない

Task 1 次の英文のうち、副詞に下線を引きなさい。

1. He's still waiting for you.
2. I never finished my degree.
3. Did you check them carefully?
4. That's too bad.
5. The company had only two branches.
6. Actually, I think it's Tammy's.
7. It's important to work hard.

Task 2 文意が通るように、括弧から適切な語句を選びなさい。

1. That new shampoo I've been using lately smells (**nice / nicely**).
2. You don't like this famous picture? Well, I don't like it, (**too / either**).
3. How (**long / short / soon**) can you finish the work?
4. Why did you (**come / come to**) home so early?
5. It was (**unfortunate / unfortunately**) that you couldn't accept the offer.
6. Computers used to take up entire rooms, but are now small (**to enough / enough to**) be put on desks.
7. You didn't know the room was changed to No. 505? (**Either / Neither / So**) did I.

Try the TOEFL Test!

Task TOEFL テストの Section 2 形式の問題です。
Part A では空所に適切な語句を選び、Part B では A ～ D の下線部のうち間違っているものを選びなさい。

Part A: Structure

1. Both museums are quite new, three years old and one year old -------.
   (A) respectfully
   (B) respectively
   (C) respectably
   (D) in respect
   Ⓐ Ⓑ Ⓒ Ⓓ

2. The largest and most abundant solutional caves, whose dissolution process produces a distinctive landform known as Karst, -------.
   (A) are typically located in limestone
   (B) typically limestone located are in
   (C) typically are located in limestone
   (D) are located in typically limestone
   Ⓐ Ⓑ Ⓒ Ⓓ

Part B: Written Expression

1. Many scientists believe <u>a huge impact</u> some 65 million years <u>ago</u> <u>triggered</u> the
                       A   B   C

   <u>known best</u> of the mass extinction of dinosaurs.
      D
   Ⓐ Ⓑ Ⓒ Ⓓ

2. The rapid extension of rail mileage enabled the railroads to <u>significant</u> <u>reduce</u>
                                                      A   B

   <u>their</u> costs for shipping <u>freight</u> and carrying passengers.
    C   D
   Ⓐ Ⓑ Ⓒ Ⓓ

3. A honey-bee society <u>usually is composed</u> of a characteristic hierarchy <u>which has</u>
                           A   B

   a population <u>of</u> 30,000 <u>to</u> 40,000 workers and one adult queen.
              C   D
   Ⓐ Ⓑ Ⓒ Ⓓ

4. Hermit crabs occupy the empty shells of dead sea snails for protection while

   <u>still retain</u> their mobility, <u>and moreover,</u> <u>they</u> change shells <u>as</u> they grow.
    A   B   C   D
   Ⓐ Ⓑ Ⓒ Ⓓ

Financial Crises

Unit 7 では経済危機について書かれたパッセージを読んでいきます。取り上げられているのは、経済危機が環境に及ぼす影響についてです。

Task 1 以下のパッセージを読みなさい。

Task 2 時間を意識して右の設問を解きなさい。理想は、設問ひとつにつき 1 分以内で解けることですが、今回は 10 分程度にタイマーを設定し、5 問以上の正解を目指します。

   * Task は順に学習しても、p. 54 の Vocabulary Check! を先に行ってからでも構いません。

 Track 42

A worldwide financial crisis has innumerable effects, and while it is impossible to document all individual hardships, it is possible to ponder some of the more general ones. Although it is hotly debated, among the possible effects that could touch all of us is how a slowing economy influences the global environment. At first, it may seem that diminished economic activity would help the environment because of lower *5* consumption, but the long-term effects might be quite different.

Optimists argue that a global financial crisis is good for the environment because the demand for natural resources and fuel use are reduced along with lower economic activity. For example, consumers are less likely to purchase new products like automobiles and televisions, but rather use existing ones longer. Furthermore, *10* rapidly developing nations like China and India require significant amounts of natural resources and produce pollution, but as economic activity slows, so does damage to the environment. Optimists consider a bad economy to be good for the environment, even if it is short-term.

On the other hand, pessimists believe that, because investment in ecological *15* products and alternative energy sources diminishes, economic recessions actually impede long-term rehabilitation of the environment. When profits are negative, companies may not have the funds to research and develop "green" products which are better for the environment. Also, investment in discovering cleaner sources of energy may suffer as money dries up, as was the recent case of a huge wind energy project *20* that stalled after new investments dried up. Essentially, pessimists feel that a failing economy is actually bad for the long-term health of the environment.

Deep recessions may indeed stabilize and perhaps help improve environmental conditions in the short-term, but it is certain that when economies begin to improve, consumption will increase, which will in turn cause renewed environmental damage. It *25* seems that we may be caught in a dilemma where we need lower economic activity to improve the environment in the short-term, yet increased economic activity is needed to create long-term benefits. In essence, if economic ups and downs could be tamed, we could achieve sustainable and long-term improvement of the environment.

Task TOEFL テストの Section 3 形式の問題です。左ページのパッセージに関する 8 つの設問に挑戦しなさい。

1. How does the author arrange the article?
   (A) By giving past examples of recessions
   (B) By listing the effects of a recession
   (C) By presenting two points of view
   (D) By showing environmental disasters
   Ⓐ Ⓑ Ⓒ Ⓓ

2. According to the article, what is one effect of a financial crisis?
   (A) Fewer optimists
   (B) Reduced consumption
   (C) Increased pollution
   (D) Enlarged investment
   Ⓐ Ⓑ Ⓒ Ⓓ

3. The word "diminished" in line 5 is closest in meaning to
   (A) enhanced
   (B) reduced
   (C) increased
   (D) improved
   Ⓐ Ⓑ Ⓒ Ⓓ

4. Where in the passage does the author provide a term for ecological goods?
   (A) Line 5
   (B) Line 9
   (C) Line 18
   (D) Line 24
   Ⓐ Ⓑ Ⓒ Ⓓ

5. The word "it" in line 14 refers to
   (A) the overall demand for natural resources
   (B) one of the rapidly developing countries
   (C) a bad economy's environmental advantages
   (D) the habits of consumers during a global recession
   Ⓐ Ⓑ Ⓒ Ⓓ

6. According to the passage, what happened to a recent wind energy project?
   (A) It was postponed.
   (B) It was cancelled.
   (C) It was completed.
   (D) It was found to pollute.
   Ⓐ Ⓑ Ⓒ Ⓓ

7. The word "dilemma" in line 26 is closest in meaning to
   (A) advantage
   (B) location
   (C) attitude
   (D) problem
   Ⓐ Ⓑ Ⓒ Ⓓ

8. According to the passage, which word best describes the issue of a recession's effects on the environment?
   (A) unknown
   (B) positive
   (C) negative
   (D) debatable
   Ⓐ Ⓑ Ⓒ Ⓓ

Vocabulary Check!

Task 1 下線部に入る適切な単語を語群から選び、書き写しなさい。
その際、p. 52 のパッセージ内でどのように使われているかを参考にしなさい。

resources	alternative	recession	rehabilitation	sustainable

1. The organization played an important role in the country's _____.
2. Japan does not have many natural _____.
3. We are supportive of what is called "_____ development."
4. In times of severe _____, companies are often forced to make job cuts in order to survive.
5. Acupuncture is widely used as _____ medicine.

Task 2 次の漢字を連想させる単語を語群から選びなさい。また、単語の意味も答えなさい。

fuel	optimist	pollution	negative	pessimist

1.「楽」_____ _____
2.「悲」_____ _____
3.「燃」_____ _____
4.「汚」_____ _____
5.「否」_____ _____

Task 3 次の単語と同様の意味を持つ語群を線で結びなさい。

1. ponder　　　　•　　　• a. reduce / lessen / make smaller
2. diminish　　　•　　　• b. consider / think over / wonder
3. furthermore　•　　　• c. in addition / besides / moreover
4. impede　　　•　　　• d. hinder / disturb / hamper
5. suffer　　　　•　　　• e. become steady / firm
6. stall　　　　　•　　　• f. endure / undergo
7. stabilize　　•　　　• g. control / manage / train
8. tame　　　　•　　　• h. delay / stop / halt

Tips 単語によっては漢字1文字でイメージしやすいものがあります。日本語1語を訳として覚えるより、イメージで覚えたほうが文脈で理解しやすい場合もあります。

Building Reading Skills!

One Point Grammar

関係詞

関係詞で重要なのは次の２点です。

1. 関係代名詞と関係副詞の正確な使い分け

先行詞の種類	主格	所有格	目的格
人	who	whose	whom / who
物・事・動物	which	whose	which
人・物・事・動物	that	—	that

※関係代名詞 what は「～すること〔もの〕」という意味で、先行詞を含んでいる。

先行詞の種類	関係副詞
場所を表す語	where
時を表す語	when
理由を表す語	why
なし	how

2. 次の関係詞にも注意

She believes **whatever** you say.

Give this ticket to **whoever** wants it. ------- whoever = anyone who
whomever とはしない

This is **how** I became disappointed.

Task 1 p. 52 のパッセージから抜粋した英文です。下線部に注意し、意味を正確に理解するようにしなさい。

When economies begin to improve, consumption will increase, <u>which</u> will in turn cause renewed environmental damage. It seems that we may be caught in a dilemma <u>where</u> we need lower economic activity to improve the environment in the short-term, yet increased economic activity is needed to create long-term benefits.

Task 2 文意が通るように、括弧から適切な語句を選びなさい。

1. Alaska's vast areas of pristine nature fascinate many people (**who / which / whom**) enjoy the outdoors.

2. Black fossil bones (**who / which / whose**) are so common in many parts of Florida are heavily mineralized.

3. Tsunamis are typically caused by big, shallow earthquakes (**which / whose / whom**) epicenters are on the ocean floor.

4. The National Zoological Park was created in Washington, D.C. (**when / where / what**) zoo animals live in natural groupings rather than as individuals.

Task 3 A ～ D の下線部のうち、間違っている個所を指摘しなさい。また、その訂正方法も答えなさい。

1. In 1930, American <u>astronomer</u> Clyde Tombaugh <u>discovered</u> the dwarf planet Pluto <u>where</u>
                A   **B**   **C**

   existence <u>had earlier been predicted</u> by Percival Lowell.
               D

   (   ) ⇒ _____

2. Kyphosis, an excessive outward curvature of the spine, <u>is</u> common <u>among</u> older people
                                                  A   **B**

   <u>to whom</u> <u>have not exercised</u> regularly throughout their lives.
       C   **D**

   (   ) ⇒ _____

3. Antique collecting became popular in the 1800s <u>which</u> old craftwork <u>began to</u> be
                                             A   **B**

   appreciated for its beauty <u>as well as</u> for its <u>historical</u> importance.
                         C   **D**

   (   ) ⇒ _____

4. I'd like to give you <u>some</u> historical facts <u>that</u> might help you <u>appreciate</u> <u>which</u> you see
                            A   **B**   **C**   **D**

   today.

   (   ) ⇒ _____

Try the TOEFL Test!

Task TOEFL テストの Section 2 形式の問題です。

Part A では空所に適切な語句を選び、Part B では A ～ D の下線部のうち間違っているものを選びなさい。

Part A: Structure

1. Every ice crystal has a minuscule core, a solid particle of matter ------- moisture condenses and freezes.
   (A) around whose
   (B) around which
   (C) around what
   (D) around whom

   Ⓐ Ⓑ Ⓒ Ⓓ

2. While all aging adults have some neurofibrillary tangles, ------- Alzheimer's disease have far more.
   (A) to whom show symptoms of
   (B) those who show symptoms of
   (C) is showing symptoms of
   (D) the reason why symptoms of

   Ⓐ Ⓑ Ⓒ Ⓓ

Part B: Written Expression

1. One study reported <u>that</u> people <u>were</u> teenagers <u>during</u> the Great Depression of
                       A   B   C

   the 1930s <u>showed</u> fewer long-term effects.
            D

   Ⓐ Ⓑ Ⓒ Ⓓ

2. <u>In</u> the United States, a primary election <u>is</u> an important process <u>by what</u> voters
   A   B   C

   <u>select</u> nominees for public office.
      D

   Ⓐ Ⓑ Ⓒ Ⓓ

3. In the mid-nineteenth century, Europe began to send <u>a number of</u> immigrants——most
                                                  A

   <u>in whom</u> were originally poor farmers but <u>who</u> <u>settled</u> in American industrial cities.
    B   C   D

   Ⓐ Ⓑ Ⓒ Ⓓ

4. In humans, Anaerobic bacteria <u>that</u> can live or grow only <u>there</u> is no oxygen <u>are</u>
                                   A   B   C

   <u>most</u> commonly found in the gastrointestinal tract.
    D

   Ⓐ Ⓑ Ⓒ Ⓓ

Conversation between a Professor and a Student

Unit 8 では、学生と教授の会話を題材にします。学生が何に悩み、教授がどのようにアドバイスをしているのか注意して聞きましょう。

Try the TOEFL Test!

Task TOEFL テストの Section 1: Part B 形式の問題です。
長めの会話文を聞き、その内容に関する 5 つの設問に答えなさい。

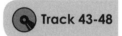 **Track 43-48**

1. (A) A grade on a term paper.
   (B) Advice about books to read.
   (C) Topics for a report.
   (D) Racism in a university.

   ⒶⒷⒸⒹ

2. (A) Literature.
   (B) Economics.
   (C) Racial issues.
   (D) Discrimination issues.

   ⒶⒷⒸⒹ

3. (A) The mid-twentieth century.
   (B) The early twentieth century.
   (C) The late nineteenth century.
   (D) The late twentieth century.

   ⒶⒷⒸⒹ

4. (A) Racial unfairness.
   (B) Economic change.
   (C) Race and identity.
   (D) Economic inequality.

   ⒶⒷⒸⒹ

5. (A) *King Coal.*
   (B) *The Jungle.*
   (C) *The Profits of Religion.*
   (D) *Native Son.*

   ⒶⒷⒸⒹ

Building Listening Skills!

Task 1 左ページの英文音声を聞き、次の質問に答えなさい。できるだけ英語で答えること。

Q1. What is the student's problem?

_____

Q2. What are the two most popular topics to write about?

_____

Task 2 左ページの会話文です。
音声を聞き、下線部に入る語句を書き取りなさい。

A: Hello, Professor Carlson. Would it be OK to talk to you about ①_____
for a few minutes?

B: I have to go to a meeting at 1:00, but I can give you ②_____
of my time. Please come in.

A: Thank you. I'm having a problem deciding ③_____
and thought you could give me some advice.

B: That seems to be rather common this term. Maybe ④_____
or I have a group of students that just can't make decisions.

A: I think ⑤_____. Well, I really can't decide whether to write
about a story that has a lot of economic issues or one with racial issues.

B: Both of those topics are ⑥_____. If you write a paper about
economic issues, which book will you ⑦_____?

A: I was thinking about *The Jungle, King Coal*, or *The Profits of Religion* by Upton
Sinclair. I know they were written just ⑧_____ in the twentieth century,
but I'm interested in the way he showed social inequality ⑨_____
_____ and what effects it had on society.

B: That would be a good topic, but it might be a little broad for the midterm report.
⑩_____ for the final paper?

A: I see ⑪_____. That's probably a better idea.

B: So, what's your idea about a paper ⑫_____?

A: I'm thinking about writing something on *Native Son* by Richard Wright. I'd like to
show ⑬_____ throughout the story
because of the discrimination he felt. Does that sound possible?

B: ⑭_____ than your first one. Why don't
you write about that?

A: OK. I'll do it. Thank you for your time today.

B: You're welcome. Good luck with the paper.

Speaking

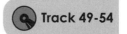
Track 49-54

Task 1 p. 58 の英文のうち、重要な個所を抜粋しています。
まず、英文を見ながら、音声に合せて、音読しなさい。

Task 2 [ペア・ワーク] ペアになって、速く正確に読む競争をしなさい。1 回目は同時にスタートし、2 回目は
負けた人が先にスタートし、2 文目の rather common まで来たら、勝った人が追いかけなさい。

Task 3 慣れてきたら右側の日本語だけを見て、英語でスラスラ言えるようになるまで練習しなさい。

English	Japanese
A: I'm having a problem deciding what to write about. B: That seems to be rather common this term.	A: 何について書くかを決めるのに困っています。 B: それは今学期、みんなの問題みたいですね。
A: I really can't decide whether to write about economic issues or racial issues. B: Both of those topics are fairly popular.	A: 経済問題を書くか、人種問題を書くか、決められません。 B: どちらのトピックも、まあよく書かれますね。
A: I'm interested in the way he showed social inequality between the rich and the poor. B: That would be a good topic, but it might be a little broad for the midterm report.	A: 私は、富裕層と貧困層の社会的不平等さを示した彼の方法に関心があります。 B: それはよいトピックでしょうが、中間のレポートとしては、少し幅広いかもしれませんね。
B: What's your idea about a paper on racism? A: I'd like to show how the main character changed because of the discrimination he felt.	B: あなたの、人種差別に関する論文についてのアイディアは何ですか。 A: 私が示したいのは、主人公が感じた差別のために性格がどのように変わったかです。
A: Does that sound possible? B: That sounds like a better idea than your first one.	A: それは可能でしょうか。 B: それは、最初のアイディアより、いいようですね。
B: Why don't you write about that? A: OK. I'll do it. Thank you for your time today.	B: それについて書いてはどうですか。 A: わかりました。そうします。お時間をいただき、ありがとうございました。

Vocabulary Check!

Task 主な学問名を、それぞれ語群から選び書き込みなさい。

I.

aesthetics	art	ethics	linguistics
literature	philosophy	theology	

1. 哲学 ＿＿＿＿＿＿＿＿　　5. 倫理学 ＿＿＿＿＿＿＿＿
2. 神学 ＿＿＿＿＿＿＿＿　　6. 言語学 ＿＿＿＿＿＿＿＿
3. 文学 ＿＿＿＿＿＿＿＿　　7. 美学 ＿＿＿＿＿＿＿＿
4. 芸術 ＿＿＿＿＿＿＿＿

II.

anthropology	archaeology	economics	ethnology
jurisprudence	history	politics	sociology

1. 歴史 ＿＿＿＿＿＿＿＿　　5. 政治学 ＿＿＿＿＿＿＿＿
2. 社会学 ＿＿＿＿＿＿＿＿　　6. 考古学 ＿＿＿＿＿＿＿＿
3. 民族学 ＿＿＿＿＿＿＿＿　　7. 人類学 ＿＿＿＿＿＿＿＿
4. 経済学 ＿＿＿＿＿＿＿＿　　8. 法学 ＿＿＿＿＿＿＿＿

III.

accounting	astronomy	biology	botany	geology
geography	mathematics	meteorology	oceanography	
physics	statistics	zoology		

1. 数学 ＿＿＿＿＿＿＿＿　　7. 統計学 ＿＿＿＿＿＿＿＿
2. 会計学 ＿＿＿＿＿＿＿＿　　8. 地質学 ＿＿＿＿＿＿＿＿
3. 地理学 ＿＿＿＿＿＿＿＿　　9. 気象学 ＿＿＿＿＿＿＿＿
4. 海洋学 ＿＿＿＿＿＿＿＿　　10. 動物学 ＿＿＿＿＿＿＿＿
5. 植物学 ＿＿＿＿＿＿＿＿　　11. 生物学 ＿＿＿＿＿＿＿＿
6. 物理学 ＿＿＿＿＿＿＿＿　　12. 天文学 ＿＿＿＿＿＿＿＿

Tips 学問名には最後にsがついているものが多いですが、単数扱いになることを覚えておきましょう。

One Point Grammar

One Point Grammar

準動詞

準動詞では、とくに次の 4 つの点に気をつけます。

- -

1. ing 形と to 不定詞の使い分け：動詞によって正確に使い分ける。
   ① ing 形を用いる主な動詞
      avoid / deny / enjoy / finish / mind / put off (= postpone) / stop など
   ② to 不定詞を用いる主な動詞
      afford / decide / expect / fail / hesitate / hope / refuse / want / wish など
   ③ どちらも用いるが、意味が変わる動詞
      forget / remember / stop など
2. 〈have ＋人＋動詞の原形〉と〈have ＋物＋過去分詞〉
3. 重要構文〈It is ～（for ＋人）to ...〉＝〈It is ～ that ...〉
   It is natural **for you to** have different opinions from your parents.
   ＝ **It is** natural **that** you should have different opinions from your parents.
4. 分詞構文における主語の扱い：主語が一致しない場合は、必ずその主語を示す。
   Being tired, I went to bed early.-------- 主語が一致
   I will go to the mountainside, <u>weather</u> **permitting**.-------- 主語が不一致⇒ weather が必要
   [誤] Walking on the street, a good idea struck me.
   ⇒ [正] Walking on the street, I came up with a good idea.

Task 1 文意が通るように、括弧から適切な語句を選びなさい。

1. Daniel has almost finished **(to write / writing)** the essay.
2. Did you enjoy **(to sing / singing)** with your friends?
3. If you failed **(to submit / submitting)** the report, you won't get any credit.
4. I am sorry to have kept you **(to wait / waiting)** for so long.

Task 2 次のふたつの文が同様の意味になるように空所に適切な語句を入れなさい。

1. Whenever I go to the Student Affairs Office, there's always a huge line.
   ＝ I never go to the Student Affairs Office ＿＿＿＿＿＿ ＿＿＿＿＿＿ a huge line.
2. May I borrow that newspaper?
   ＝ Do you mind my ＿＿＿＿＿＿ that newspaper?
3. The earthquake was so strong that it caused topographical changes in that area.
   ＝ The earthquake was strong ＿＿＿＿＿＿ ＿＿＿＿＿＿ cause topographical
   changes in the area.
4. As I didn't know what to do about this, I came to you for advice.
   ＝ ＿＿＿＿＿＿ ＿＿＿＿＿＿ what to do about this, I came to you for advice.

Try the TOEFL Test!

Task TOEFL テストの Section 2 形式の問題です。

Part A では空所に適切な語句を選び、Part B では A ～ D の下線部のうち間違っているものを選びなさい。

Part A: Structure

1. Although we wanted a casual gathering, Gary insisted ------- the party at a decent hotel.
(A) on having
(B) to have
(C) for having
(D) that having

2. I remember ------- wooden floors, therefore they were easily damaged by heavy   Ⓐ Ⓑ Ⓒ Ⓓ
machinery and fire.
(A) to read that factories had
(B) read that factories made
(C) because of factories
(D) reading that factories used to have

Ⓐ Ⓑ Ⓒ Ⓓ

Part B: Written Expression

1. Why do you think <u>it is</u> so <u>surprised</u> that early humans had <u>detailed</u> knowledge
      A   B   C

about <u>plants</u>?
  D   Ⓐ Ⓑ Ⓒ Ⓓ

2. I saw <u>a full</u> circle <u>of</u> rainbow hues <u>was hanging</u> in the sky just <u>above</u> the sea. Ⓐ Ⓑ Ⓒ Ⓓ
    A   B   C   D

3. The farmers were not <u>interesting</u> in cast-iron plows, <u>claiming</u> that iron
          A   B

<u>poisoned</u> the <u>soil</u>.
  C   D   Ⓐ Ⓑ Ⓒ Ⓓ

4. The use of products <u>containing</u> CFCs (artificial chemicals) allows them <u>to enter</u>
           A   B

the atmosphere, <u>caused</u> the depletion <u>of</u> the ozone layer.
      C   D   Ⓐ Ⓑ Ⓒ Ⓓ

Native Americans

Unit 9 では、ネイティブ・アメリカンのカジノ経営について書かれたパッセージを読んでいきます。

Task 1 以下のパッセージを読みなさい。

Task 2 時間を意識して右の設問を解きなさい。理想は、設問ひとつにつき 1 分以内で解けることですが、今回は
13 分程度にタイマーを設定し、7 問以上の正解を目指します。

＊Task は順に学習しても、p. 66 の Vocabulary Check! を先に行ってからでも構いません。

 Track 55

There are currently 562 federally recognized Native American tribes in the United States of America and approximately 220 of them offer casino gambling on their lands. However, despite the recent popularity and successes of Native American casinos, there has been substantial legal conflict with state governments and controversy over whether gambling operations benefit or harm Native Americans. 5

An early example of gambling operations on Native American lands is with the Cabazon, a subgroup of Mission Indians in Southern California. Because the California state government neglected treaties, the Cabazon had neither much wealth nor land of which to speak. In 1980, to generate income, they turned to minor gambling operations but were soon shut down by local law enforcement agencies. Numerous Cabazon 10 Indians were arrested, and gambling instruments and proceeds were confiscated.

The Cabazon successfully sued the state in federal courts, and in 1986, upon review with other cases, the Supreme Court declared that Indian gaming should be regulated only by the national government. In 1988, President Ronald Regan signed the Indian Gaming Regulatory Act (IGRA), which put into law that Native American 15 tribes have the right to run gambling operations. With gaming cleared of rigorous state control and tribal sovereignty protected, the way was paved for many other tribes to begin gaming operations.

After the IGRA came into effect, Indian gaming revenue coming from approximately 400 establishments soared from $100 million in 1988 to $16.7 billion in 20 2006. In addition, the Foxwoods Casino, operated by the Mashantucket Pequot Indians in Connecticut, is currently the largest gambling establishment in the nation and has brought more than $1.7 billion to the state tax system.

However, the effects of gambling operations on Native Americans are imbued with controversy. Some point out that positive results include an 11.5% population increase 25 on Indian reservations, employment increasing by 26%, a 14% decline in the working poor, and a decline in the mortality rate. Others maintain that negative changes include 10% increases in auto theft, robbery, and violent crimes, and increased bankruptcies in and around casinos. In addition, some say that most casino employees are not Native Americans and that casinos, whose profits are by and large tax-free, take urgently 30 needed funds away from state governments.

Notwithstanding the controversy over legal, moral, or economic implications of gambling operations on Native American lands, the steady increases of such ventures suggest that they will continue to flourish in the foreseeable future.

Try the TOEFL Test!

Task TOEFL テストの Section 3 形式の問題です。左ページのパッセージに関する 10 の設問に挑戦しなさい。

1. What is the main point of this article?
   (A) Indian casinos are helping the national government.
   (B) Legal challenges have harmed Native American societies.
   (C) Effects of Indian casinos are good for all.
   (D) Gambling money has improved Native American's lives.
   ⒶⒷⒸⒹ

2. The word "operations" in line 6 is closest in meaning to
   (A) judgments
   (B) failures
   (C) citizens
   (D) businesses
   ⒶⒷⒸⒹ

3. According to the article, about how many different Native American groups offer casino gaming?
   (A) 220
   (B) 560
   (C) 400
   (D) 100
   ⒶⒷⒸⒹ

4. The word "confiscated" in line 11 is closest in meaning to
   (A) broken
   (B) taken
   (C) counted
   (D) given
   ⒶⒷⒸⒹ

5. In which year did federal judges declare Indian casinos free from state control?
   (A) 1980
   (B) 1986
   (C) 1988
   (D) 2006
   ⒶⒷⒸⒹ

6. The word "sovereignty" in line 17 is closest in meaning to
   (A) support
   (B) business
   (C) accounts
   (D) independence
   ⒶⒷⒸⒹ

7. What does the author suggest was unclear about gaming on Native American lands in the past?
   (A) How many of them should exist in certain areas.
   (B) Whether non-Native Americans could also be employed.
   (C) Who should control them.
   (D) What types of gambling should be allowed.
   ⒶⒷⒸⒹ

8. The word "maintain" in line 27 is closest in meaning to
   (A) believe
   (B) continue
   (C) disagree
   (D) remain
   ⒶⒷⒸⒹ

9. Which is NOT mentioned as a benefit of Indian casinos?
   (A) Increased job rates
   (B) A rising population
   (C) Expanded Indian lands
   (D) Decreased death rates
   ⒶⒷⒸⒹ

10. What does the author suggest about the future of casinos on Native American lands?
    (A) Smaller ones will be developed.
    (B) They will continue to be popular.
    (C) Governments will become stricter with them.
    (D) States will continue to legally challenge them.
    ⒶⒷⒸⒹ

Vocabulary Check!

Task 1 p. 64 のパッセージから、次の意味を持つ単語を探し出し、書き写しなさい。

1. およそ、約〜 _____ = nearly / almost
2. 法律の _____ = allowed or approved by law
3. 非常に多くの _____ = many / myriad
4. 暴力的な _____ = dangerous / damaging
5. 安定した _____ = not moving / continuous
6. 道徳的な _____ = about what is right and wrong
7. 予測できる _____ = expected / probable

Task 2 下線部に入る適切な単語を語群から選び、書き写しなさい。
p. 64 のパッセージでどのように使われているかも参考にしなさい。

generate	arrested	confiscated	sue	maintains

1. The manufacturer _____ that product quality is their top priority.
2. Dams are used to control flooding and _____ electricity.
3. Cameras may be _____ if they are used inside this building.
4. The police finally _____ the politician for bribery.
5. Mrs. Smart is going to _____ her boss for sexual harassment.

Task 3 次の単語と、その定義文、もしくは同様の意味を持つ語群を線で結びなさい。

1. tribe •　　　• **a.** being unable to pay debts
2. conflict •　　　• **b.** income / earnings
3. treaty •　　　• **c.** group / community / race
4. sovereignty •　　　• **d.** quarrel / disagreement
5. revenue •　　　• **e.** relation / effect
6. bankruptcy •　　　• **f.** a business activity involving risks
7. implication •　　　• **g.** agreement / protocol
8. venture •　　　• **h.** governance / rule

Building Reading Skills!

One Point Grammar

受動態

受動態で重要なのは次の4つです。

． ．

1. 受動態の形 〈be 動詞＋過去分詞〉

   A stranger spoke to me. ⇒ **I was spoken** to by a stranger.

   Satoshi gave Makoto a book. ⇒ Makoto **was given** a book by Satoshi.

   A book **was given** to Makoto by Satoshi.

   ※ give / tell / show / teach など、目的語をふたつ取る動詞は2通りの受動態を作る。

2. 進行形の受動態 〈be 動詞＋ being ＋過去分詞〉

   The guard is watching the prisoner. ⇒ The prisoner **is being watched** by the guard.

3. 能動態には不要だが、受動態には必要となる前置詞に注意

   My father made me stay home. ⇒ I was made **to** stay home by my father.

   My parents never let me stay out overnight.

   ⇒ I was never allowed by my parents **to** stay out overnight.

4. 受動態にした場合、落としやすい前置詞に注意

   Classmates laughed at the boys. ⇒ The boys were laughed **at** by classmates.

   Everyone looked up to the leader. ⇒ The leader was looked up **to** by everyone.

Task 1 p. 64 のパッセージから抜粋した英文です。下線部に注意し、意味を正確に理解するようにしなさい。

1. There are currently 562 federally <u>recognized</u> Native American tribes in the United States of America.

2. Numerous Cabazon Indians <u>were arrested</u>, and gambling instruments and proceeds <u>were confiscated</u>.

3. With gaming <u>cleared</u> of rigorous state control and tribal sovereignty <u>protected</u>, the way <u>was paved</u> for many other tribes to begin gaming operations.

Task 2 文意が通るように、括弧から適切な語句を選びなさい。

1. Foster's music (**describes / is described / is describing**) as a hybrid of blues, gospel, and folk music.

2. A delightful sparkling wine, Champagne is (**name / named / naming**) after a region in northern France.

3. Industrialization has been responsible for the most serious environmental changes (**cause / caused / causing**) by humans.

4. The body of a reptile is protected because the skin is (**covered at / covered with / covered for**) plates or scales, which prevents evaporation and therefore dehydration.

Task 3 A ~ D の下線部のうち、間違っている個所を指摘しなさい。また、その訂正方法も答えなさい。

1. One of the <u>most characteristic</u> differences <u>between</u> sleep and hibernation <u>seen</u> in body
   　　　　　　　A　　　　　　　　　　　　B　　　　　　　　　　　　　　C

   temperatures <u>and</u> heart rates.
   　　　　　　　D

   (　　　　) ⇒＿＿＿＿＿＿＿＿＿＿＿＿＿

2. Machine tools, which <u>use</u> to <u>make</u> goods in modern factory lines, <u>were steadily improved</u>
   　　　　　　　　　　A　　　B　　　　　　　　　　　　　　　　　　C

   in the <u>latter</u> half of the nineteenth century.
   　　　　D

   (　　　　) ⇒＿＿＿＿＿＿＿＿＿＿＿＿＿

3. Skin cancer is <u>a</u> malignant growth on the skin and <u>it</u> has been <u>reported to</u> be directly
   　　　　　　　A　　　　　　　　　　　　　　　B　　　　　　C

   <u>link to</u> sun exposure and damage.
   　D

   (　　　　) ⇒＿＿＿＿＿＿＿＿＿＿＿＿＿

4. <u>With</u> budgets for public works <u>drastically slashing</u>, a huge number of <u>jobs</u>
   　A　　　　　　　　　　　　　　B　　　　　　　　　　　　　　C

   have <u>been eliminated</u> in the construction industry.
   　　　　D

   (　　　　) ⇒＿＿＿＿＿＿＿＿＿＿＿＿＿

Try the TOEFL Test!

(Task) TOEFL テストの Section 2 形式の問題です。

Part A では空所に適切な語句を選び、Part B では A ～ D の下線部のうち間違っているものを選びなさい。

Part A: Structure

1. The color of blood is strongly ------- to the blood cells that transport oxygen.
   (A) relate
   (B) relation of
   (C) relating
   (D) related

   Ⓐ Ⓑ Ⓒ Ⓓ

2. Generally speaking, an individual who dresses smartly and shows self-confidence
   ------- capable of doing a job well regardless of his or her real ability.
   (A) is likely to be judging
   (B) likely to be judged
   (C) is likely to be judged
   (D) to be likely judged

   Ⓐ Ⓑ Ⓒ Ⓓ

Part B: Written Expression

1. A mineral can <u>defined</u> as an inorganic solid that <u>occurs</u> naturally and <u>possesses</u>
          A   B   C

   a systematic structure and a specific <u>chemical composition</u>.
                                        D

   Ⓐ Ⓑ Ⓒ Ⓓ

2. Narcissus bulbs <u>should be</u> planted <u>at least</u> three inches apart and <u>cover</u> with
                A   B   C

   about four inches <u>of</u> moist soil.
                    D

   Ⓐ Ⓑ Ⓒ Ⓓ

3. The tree <u>on</u> the grounds of the university <u>said</u> to <u>have been</u> the inspiration <u>for</u>
        A   B   C   D

   Joyce Kilmer's poem "Trees."

   Ⓐ Ⓑ Ⓒ Ⓓ

4. <u>Recognizing</u> as the oldest freshwater lake on the planet, Lake Baikal is also
       A

   <u>measured</u> as the deepest continental body of water, <u>holding</u> the water of all the
       B   C

   Great Lakes <u>combined</u>.
               D

   Ⓐ Ⓑ Ⓒ Ⓓ

Unit 10

The Civil War

Unit 10 では The Civil War（南北戦争）に関する講義を聞きます。

Try the TOEFL Test!

(Task) TOEFL テストの Section 1: Part C 形式の問題です。
長めの英文を聞き、その内容に関する 4 つの設問に答えなさい。

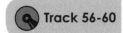 **Track 56-60**

1. (A) How the Union imported European goods.
   (B) How agriculture was considerably transformed.
   (C) How the population moved from south to north.
   (D) How important resources were to winning it.

   Ⓐ Ⓑ Ⓒ Ⓓ

2. (A) 25 percent.
   (B) 70 percent.
   (C) 50 percent.
   (D) 30 percent.

   Ⓐ Ⓑ Ⓒ Ⓓ

3. (A) Offered it a bigger share of exports.
   (B) Made a peace agreement with the Union.
   (C) Stopped its cotton shipments.
   (D) Tried to grow more grain for export.

   Ⓐ Ⓑ Ⓒ Ⓓ

4. (A) They had a shortage of cotton.
   (B) Their economies were beginning to improve.
   (C) Their citizens were against slavery.
   (D) The Union depended on them for food.

   Ⓐ Ⓑ Ⓒ Ⓓ

Building Listening Skills!

Task 1 左ページの英文音声を聞き、次の質問に答えなさい。できるだけ英語で答えること。

Q1. Who fought the Civil War?

_____

Q2. Who won the Civil War?

_____

Task 2 左ページの英文です。
音声を聞き、下線部に入る語句を書き取りなさい。

Historians often ① _____ the northern Union's American Civil War victory over the southern Confederacy to the ② _____ _____ it possessed. For example, the Union had more than sixteen million people and one million more soldiers than the Confederacy. Of course ③ _____ helped win battlefield victories, but the much higher total population helped the Union produce considerably more than the Confederacy. In fact, the North ④ _____ more than nine times that of the South.

On the other hand, the Confederacy's share of pre-war exports was ⑤ _____ of the U.S. total compared to only ⑥ _____ for the Union. Southerners of the Confederacy knew this and tried to use it ⑦ _____ by blockading shipments of cotton, their largest crop. They did this ⑧ _____ creating economic trouble in Europe that would force Britain to enter the war to obtain raw materials from the North American continent.

However, ⑨ _____ stopped this from ever happening. The first was that Europe had ⑩ _____ at the time and needed little of it from the Confederacy. Also, European ⑪ _____ between 1860 to 1862 made grain imports from the Union of utmost importance. These types of imports increased from ⑫ _____ during the Civil War, creating a dependency on the Union's agriculture. Economic reliance, ⑬ _____ _____, made politicians reluctant to associate with the cotton producing, slave owning southern states of the Confederacy.

Speaking

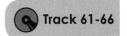

Track 61-66

(Task 1) p. 70 の英文のうち、重要な個所を抜粋しています。

まず、英文を見ながら、音声に合せて、音読しなさい。

(Task 2) [ペア・ワーク] ペアになって、速く正確に読む競争をしなさい。1回目は同時にスタートし、2回目は

負けた人が先にスタートし、2文目の The Union had まで来たら、勝った人が追いかけなさい。

(Task 3) 慣れてきたら右側の日本語だけを見て、英文をスラスラ読めるようになるまで練習しなさい。

English	Japanese
Historians attribute the northern Union's victory over the Confederacy to its human and material resources.	歴史家は、北部連合軍が南部連合軍に勝ったのは、その人的資源と物資のおかげだとしている。
The Union had one million more soldiers than the Confederacy.	北軍は南軍より 100 万人以上兵士が多かった。
The North manufactured more than nine times that of the South.	北軍は南軍の 9 倍以上を生産した。
They knew this and tried to use it to their advantage.	彼らはこれを知っていて、自分たちに有利になるよう利用しようとした。
They did this in the hopes of creating economic trouble in Europe.	彼らは、ヨーロッパに経済問題を引き起こそうと思って、これを行った。
Three main factors stopped this from ever happening.	3つの主な要因が、これが起こることを阻止した。

Vocabulary Check!

Task 1 次の単語と、その定義を線で結びなさい。

1. attribute   •   • **a.** something very impressive or greatly affecting you
2. overwhelming   •   • **b.** to make goods, usually using machines
3. possess   •   • **c.** being unwilling and slow
4. manufacture   •   • **d.** to say A is caused by B
5. surplus   •   • **e.** the state of needing help and support
6. reluctant   •   • **f.** the amount of something more than needed
7. dependence   •   • **g.** to own something, usually valuable

Task 2 次の空所に適切な語を **Task 1** から選び、かつ〈　〉に適切な前置詞を入れなさい。

1. The government wants to reduce its _____ 〈　　　〉 foreign oil.
2. Educational experts _____ the problems of those children 〈　　　〉 their parents.
3. Mr. Whitfield seems _____ 〈　　　〉 go into detail about the origin of the ritual.

> **Tips**
> 一定の前置詞と一緒に用いられる単語は、このように文で覚えるようにしましょう。

One Point Grammar

One Point Grammar

前置詞

前置詞で注意すべき点は次のふたつです。

1. 次の用法に注意
   ① till ～と by ～
      Wait here **till** I come back. / Finish it **by** five.
   ② known to ～ / known as ～ / known for ～ / known by ～
   ③ made of ～ / made from ～
   ④ result in ～ / result from ～
   ⑤ provide 人 with 物 ＝ provide 物 for 人
   ⑥ compare A with B / compare A to B
   ⑦ familiar with 物 / familiar to 人
      I'm familiar **with** it. ＝ It's familiar **to** me.

2. 前置詞を伴わない他動詞に注意
   discuss / mention / enter / reach / explain など

Task 1 文意が通るように、空所に適切な前置詞を入れなさい。

1. How can you tell a real diamond _____ a fake one?

2. Your voice is so similar _____ your mother's that I can't tell them apart.

3. Dr. Sanson looks very young _____ her age.

4. More than one hundred people participated _____ the seminar.

5. The meeting will start _____ ten o'clock.

6. _____ my surprise, he failed the interview test.

7. It gets very cold here _____ February.

8. Most schools start _____ April 8 _____ Japan.

Task 2 次の文にある間違いに下線を引き、訂正方法を答えなさい。

1. I was surprised about the news.　　　　⇒ _____

2. We enjoyed dancing with the music.　　⇒ _____

3. My brother got injured from a traffic accident.　⇒ _____

4. She was robbed her bag on the street.　⇒ _____

5. Because these reasons, I like living in the countryside, not in urban areas.

　　　　　　　　　　　　　　　　　　⇒ _____

Try the TOEFL Test!

Task TOEFL テストの Section 2 形式の問題です。

Part A では空所に適切な語句を選び、Part B では A ～ D の下線部のうち間違っているものを選びなさい。

Part A: Structure

1. The professor concluded that the depth marked the boundary ------- a solid
   mantle and a liquid core.
   (A) among
   (B) between
   (C) during
   (D) while

   Ⓐ Ⓑ Ⓒ Ⓓ

2. The author mentioned these two valleys ------- of those in the north and those
   in the south of the country.
   (A) when comparing with the characteristics
   (B) compared to characteristics
   (C) to compare the characteristics
   (D) to be compared the characteristics

   Ⓐ Ⓑ Ⓒ Ⓓ

Part B: Written Expression

1. <u>According by</u> the police, the fire <u>that</u> claimed many <u>lives</u> started <u>in</u> the restaurant.
       A   B   C   D

   Ⓐ Ⓑ Ⓒ Ⓓ

2. The <u>detailed</u> global investigation <u>of</u> the ocean bottom did not actually start
         A   B

   <u>during</u> the end <u>of</u> 1968.
      C   D

   Ⓐ Ⓑ Ⓒ Ⓓ

3. <u>For</u> those of you staying <u>behind</u> the campground, make sure that you <u>set up</u>
    A   B   C

   camp away <u>from</u> poisonous plants.
             D

   Ⓐ Ⓑ Ⓒ Ⓓ

4. It can be inferred <u>from</u> the passage that middle-income people <u>in</u> the United States
                          A   B

   <u>tend to</u> prefer living closer to urban amenities <u>than</u> residing in the countryside.
     C   D

   Ⓐ Ⓑ Ⓒ Ⓓ

An Environmental Problem

Unit 11 は、現在大きな問題のひとつである環境についてです。温暖化、動物保護などの記事は、日頃から
インターネットなどを利用して、英語で読んだり聞いたりしておきましょう。

Task 1 以下のパッセージを読みなさい。

Task 2 時間を意識して右の設問を解きなさい。理想は、設問ひとつにつき 1 分以内で解けることですが、今回は
15 分程度にタイマーを設定し、7 問以上の正解を目指します。

　＊ Task は順に学習しても、p. 78 の Vocabulary Check! を先に行ってからでも構いません。

Track 67

　　Although the phenomena of global warming is gaining acceptance and former
skeptics are now acknowledging that worldwide temperatures are on the rise, its effects
are far from predictable. One prime example is the tremendously large ice sheet on
the continent of Antarctica, whose vast reserves of frozen water could have a very
significant effect on rising sea levels.　　　　　　　　　　　　　　　　　　　　　　　5

　　According to many estimates, Antarctica has 90% of the earth's ice reserves and
80% of the world's fresh water, and if extensive melting of this ice were to occur,
catastrophic rises in sea levels would take place. This is why so much research has been
dedicated to whether the overall Antarctic ice sheet has been melting.

　　Melting sea ice (called so because it extends from the land onto the sea)——most　10
notably on the Wilkins ice shelf——has been observed in parts of the west Antarctic
region. This melting has caused calvings (pieces of ice breaking off) on a significant
scale, which leads some to believe that melting Antarctic ice is leading to sea level
rises. In fact, some experts have predicted a 6-meter rise from Antarctic melting by
2100.　　　　　　　　　　　　　　　　　　　　　　　　　　　　　　　　　　　　15

　　On the other hand, other specialists have stated that there may only be a 1.25-meter
rise and still others assert that the magnitude of ice breaking off may not be unusual at
all. According to one scientist, icebergs of 100 to 200 kilometers long may break off
West Antarctica in a normal cycle of 10, 20, or 50 years.

　　In addition, significant data about Antarctica's contribution to rising sea levels has　20
been found in the eastern region, which is four times the size of the west and has been
found to actually be cooling. Ice core drilling in East Antarctica has shown that the
average ice thickness has risen from 1.67 meters in the 1950s to 1.89 at present. This
suggests that losses in the western region over the past 30 years have been more than
offset by increases in the east and that the area of sea ice around the entire continent　25
has in fact expanded.

　　While global warming might apparently contribute to melting Antarctic ice and
rising sea levels in one region, data from another region tells a different story. The
Antarctic example shows us that the effects of global warming are indeed complex and
unpredictable and that they might include cooling trends as well.　　　　　　　　　30

Try the TOEFL Test!

Task TOEFL テストの Section 3 形式の問題です。左ページのパッセージに関する 10 の設問に挑戦しなさい。

1. What is the main theme of this passage?
   - (A) The effects of rising sea levels on cities.
   - (B) The percentage of fresh water in Antarctica.
   - (C) The varying consequences of warming.
   - (D) The duration of normal iceberg cycles.

   Ⓐ Ⓑ Ⓒ Ⓓ

2. Which of the following is true about sea ice?
   - (A) It is found only in the Antarctic.
   - (B) It melts faster in the east.
   - (C) It is 80% salt water.
   - (D) It is connected to ground.

   Ⓐ Ⓑ Ⓒ Ⓓ

3. The word "reserves" in line 4 is closest in meaning to
   - (A) conditions
   - (B) potential
   - (C) supplies
   - (D) movements

   Ⓐ Ⓑ Ⓒ Ⓓ

4. The word "catastrophic" in line 8 is closest in meaning to
   - (A) disastrous
   - (B) doubtful
   - (C) beneficial
   - (D) slowing

   Ⓐ Ⓑ Ⓒ Ⓓ

5. What is the current average depth of ice in East Antarctica?
   - (A) 1.25 meters
   - (B) 1.67 meters
   - (C) 6 meters
   - (D) 1.89 meters

   Ⓐ Ⓑ Ⓒ Ⓓ

6. Where does the author provide a term for icebergs being created?
   - (A) Line 10
   - (B) Line 7
   - (C) Line 21
   - (D) Line 12

   Ⓐ Ⓑ Ⓒ Ⓓ

7. The word "magnitude" in line 17 is closest in meaning to
   - (A) hazard
   - (B) amount
   - (C) possibility
   - (D) temperature

   Ⓐ Ⓑ Ⓒ Ⓓ

8. What does the second paragraph mainly discuss?
   - (A) Average ice thicknesses on the continent of Antarctica.
   - (B) The effects of melting Antarctic ice on sea levels.
   - (C) How cities should prepare for rising sea levels.
   - (D) Various approaches to research on melting sea ice.

   Ⓐ Ⓑ Ⓒ Ⓓ

9. The word "offset" in line 25 is closest in meaning to
   - (A) balanced
   - (B) investigated
   - (C) overstated
   - (D) worsened

   Ⓐ Ⓑ Ⓒ Ⓓ

10. What does the author imply about Antarctica's overall sea ice?
    - (A) It might hold less fresh water by the year 2100.
    - (B) It may not contribute to rising sea levels.
    - (C) It has been melting at a faster rate than before.
    - (D) It has decreased over the past 30 years.

    Ⓐ Ⓑ Ⓒ Ⓓ

Vocabulary Check!

Task 1 イラストを参考に、次の単語の意味を答えなさい。

1. temperature

_____

2. continent

_____

3. Antarctic

_____

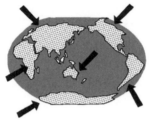

4. iceberg

_____

5. increase

_____

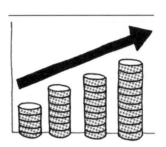

Task 2 次の単語と、それに対応する意味を線で結びなさい。

1. phenomena	•	• a. 地域
2. reserve	•	• b. 規模
3. region	•	• c. 相殺
4. magnitude	•	• d. 現象
5. contribution	•	• e. 蓄積
6. offset	•	• f. 貢献

Task 3 次の単語と同様の意味を持つ語群を線で結びなさい。

1. predict	•	• a. assessment / evaluation
2. melt	•	• b. important / meaningful
3. catastrophic	•	• c. forecast / foretell / prophesy
4. significant	•	• d. give / offer / contribute
5. estimate	•	• e. state / affirm
6. dedicate	•	• f. soften / liquefy / deform
7. observe	•	• g. devastating / unfortunate / fatal
8. assert	•	• h. watch / monitor

Tips 単語を構成している部分に注目。たとえば、predict / predictable / unpredictable の pre- は「前の」、-able は「〜できる」、un- は「〜でない」という否定の意味を持っています。

Building Reading Skills!

One Point Grammar

現在完了

現在完了は、〈have [has] ＋過去分詞〉で表し、次の３つの意味を持ちます。

1. 継続（ずっと～している）
This system **has been used** since 1950.

2. 完了（～したところだ）
The committee **has** just **changed** the system.

3. 経験（～したことがある）
They **have been** to Australia.

Task 1 p. 76 のパッセージから抜粋した英文です。下線部に注意し、意味を正確に理解するようにしなさい。

1. Significant data about Antarctica's contribution to rising sea levels <u>has been found</u> in the eastern region.

2. Ice core drilling in East Antarctica <u>has shown</u> that the average ice thickness <u>has risen</u> from 1.67 meters in the 1950s to 1.89 at present.

Task 2 文意が通るように、括弧から適切な語句を選びなさい。

1. This cave **(is / is going / has been)** under excavation since the 1940s.

2. The team **(has been excavating / is excavating / have excavated)** the cave for more than ten years.

3. The researcher **(is used / has used / is going to use)** the same approach before.

4. Five years **(has passed / have passed / had passed)** since we started this project.

Task 3 A ～ D の下線部のうち、間違っている個所を指摘しなさい。また、その訂正方法も答えなさい。

1. According to <u>a recent survey</u> conducted by a governmental institute, <u>there have been</u>
                        A   **B**

   a decrease <u>in</u> violent <u>crime</u>.
              C   **D**

   (   ) ⇒_____

2. <u>That</u> satellite <u>from</u> NASA <u>has been measuring</u> the Sun's output <u>on</u> February 1980.
   A   **B**   **C**   **D**

   (   ) ⇒_____

3. <u>Although</u> researchers <u>were formulated</u> a variety of theories to explain it, <u>why</u> certain
   A   **B**   **C**

   plants contain alkaloids <u>remains</u> a mystery.
                            D

   (   ) ⇒_____

Try the TOEFL Test!

Task TOEFL テストの Section 2 形式の問題です。
Part A では空所に適切な語句を選び、Part B では A ～ D の下線部のうち間違っているものを選びなさい。

Part A: Structure

1. A number of researchers ------- many behavioral patterns associated with selecting
   a place to live and avoiding predators.
   (A) identifies
   (B) were identified
   (C) have identified
   (D) have been identified

   Ⓐ Ⓑ Ⓒ Ⓓ

2. There ------- remarkable progress was made within a relatively short span of time.

(A) has been periods when history

(B) were periods when history was

(C) was in history when periods

(D) have been periods in history when

Ⓐ Ⓑ Ⓒ Ⓓ

1. According to a survey, <u>average</u> world temperatures <u>have</u> risen <u>by half a degree</u>
                           A   **B**   **C**

Celsius <u>during</u> the mid-nineteenth century until now.
     D
                                                    Ⓐ Ⓑ Ⓒ Ⓓ

2. This doctor's theory <u>includes</u> some aspects <u>of</u> intelligence that <u>haven't measured</u>
                             A   **B**   **C**

<u>in terms of</u> traditional intelligence testing.
    D
                                                      Ⓐ Ⓑ Ⓒ Ⓓ

3. <u>As part of</u> our research, we <u>have been collecting</u> the "extra" eggs and <u>placing</u>
     A   **B**   **C**

them in the nests of other cranes <u>since</u> more than six hours.
                               D
                                                   Ⓐ Ⓑ Ⓒ Ⓓ

4. A couple weeks ago, Dr. Anderson <u>is explained</u> that the tons of dust <u>thrown out</u>
                                        A   **B**

far into the atmosphere may <u>have caused</u> some global climate <u>change</u>.
                            C   **D**
                                                   Ⓐ Ⓑ Ⓒ Ⓓ

Astoronomy

Unit 12 では、月の誕生についての講義を聞きます。4つの仮説、それぞれの特徴に注意しましょう。

Try the TOEFL Test!

Task TOEFL テストの Section 1: Part C 形式の問題です。
長めの英文を聞き、その内容に関する5つの設問に答えなさい。

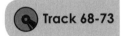
Track 68-73

1. (A) The formation of the moon.
   (B) Size differences between the Earth and the moon.
   (C) The moon's effect on the Earth.
   (D) The history of research on the Earth and the moon.

   Ⓐ Ⓑ Ⓒ Ⓓ

2. (A) The materials comprising the Earth are similar to the materials comprising
      the moon.
   (B) Mathematical calculations show that it is possible.
   (C) Collisions have happened elsewhere in the solar system.
   (D) The Earth was spinning slowly enough for it to happen.

   Ⓐ Ⓑ Ⓒ Ⓓ

3. (A) The materials comprising the moon are the same as those comprising
      the Earth.
   (B) Conditions could not have been just right.
   (C) The Earth is much bigger than the moon.
   (D) The moon's iron core would have to have been larger.

   Ⓐ Ⓑ Ⓒ Ⓓ

4. (A) It was transferred mostly to the moon.
   (B) It was spread throughout the solar system.
   (C) It mostly fell into the Earth's core.
   (D) It was the main reason for an impact.

   Ⓐ Ⓑ Ⓒ Ⓓ

5. (A) Condensation.
   (B) Capture.
   (C) Giant impact
   (D) Fission.

   Ⓐ Ⓑ Ⓒ Ⓓ

Building Listening Skills!

Task 1 左ページの英文音声を聞き、次の質問に英語で答えなさい。

Q. Write down the names of the four theories on the formation of the moon.

_____

_____

_____

_____

Task 2 再度、英文音声を聞き、次の各会話の空所に入る英文を選択肢から選びなさい。

Task 3 [ペアワーク] **Task 2** の正答を確認してから、それぞれの会話を学生と教授になったつもりで声に出して読みなさい。

〈会話〉

1. A: What does the fission theory suggest?

   B: The fission theory suggests _____.

2. A: Where does the capture theory propose the moon was formed?

   B: The capture theory proposes _____.

3. A: When does the condensation theory state the moon was formed?

   B: The condensation theory states _____.

4. A: What does the giant impactor theory state?

   B: The giant impactor theory states _____.

〈選択肢〉

a. that a huge planet-size impactor struck Earth and the moon was formed from materials ejected from the impact.

b. that the moon was formed by somehow separating from a rapidly spinning, very primitive Earth.

c. that the moon was formed at the same time as Earth was produced from the same primordial materials that formed the whole solar system.

d. that the moon was formed somewhere else in the solar system and fell into Earth orbit when it came near.

Welcome to the second lecture in our series on astronomy. As you know, today we will focus on the ①_____, and specifically ②_____. Although there are a number of theories, only one of them is widely accepted today. ③_____ are the ④_____ theory, the ⑤_____ theory, the ⑥_____ theory, and the ⑦_____ theory.

The fission theory suggests that the moon was formed by somehow ⑧_____ a rapidly spinning, very primitive ⑨_____. This theory was once thought possible because the ⑩_____. On the other hand, contemporary mathematical calculations tracing the moon's path back to Earth show that it wouldn't have been possible.

The capture theory proposes that the moon was formed ⑪_____ and ⑫_____ when it came near. Again, mathematical calculations show that, although possible, ⑬_____ that the moon could have been perfectly slowed down by the Earth's gravity AND another planet that has never been found.

The condensation theory states that ⑭_____ _____ that formed the whole solar system. Although the moon has many of the same materials as Earth, it lacks ⑮_____ that it should have if it were formed along with its mother planet.

Perhaps the most spectacular, yet widely accepted one is the giant impactor theory ⑯_____ , striking the Earth, and the moon forming materials ejected from the impact. This theory ⑰_____ with mathematical calculations, evidence of similar collisions, and the fact that heavy iron sank into Earth's core and not the moon's.

Now, I'll go into the details of each of these theories ⑱_____ in which I just mentioned them.

Vocabulary Check!

Task 1 イラストを参考に、次の単語の意味を答えなさい。

1. astronomy

2. solar

3. orbit

  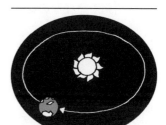

4. collision

5. evidence

6. order

Task 2 次の日本語の意味を持つ語句を語群からふたつずつ探しなさい。

be similar to	primitive	primordial	propose	resemble
suggest				

1. ～に似ている   _____   _____

2. ～を提案する、提起する   _____   _____

3. 原初の、初期の   _____   _____

Task 3 次の語句と、それに対応する定義を線で結びなさい。

1. focus •

  • **a.** a formal set of ideas that is intended to explain why something happens or exists

2. theory •

  • **b.** modern, belonging to or occurring in the present

3. fission •

  • **c.** to give special attention to one particular person or thing

4. contemporary •

  • **d.** relating to or using mathematics

5. mathematical •

  • **e.** the act or process of separating into parts

6. coalesce •

  • **f.** to come together to form one larger group, substance

7. spectacular •

  • **g.** very impressive and exciting to look at or watch

One Point Grammar

One Point Grammar

疑問詞

疑問詞で重要なのは次の2点です。

. . . .

1. 主な疑問詞

   what / which / who (whom, whose) / when / where / why / how

2. 間接疑問文の語順に注意

   I didn't know where he would go.

Task 1 下線部が答えになる疑問文を作りなさい。

1. <u>Jane</u> went to the party with me. ⇒ _____

2. This is <u>Mike's</u> book. ⇒ _____

3. I like <u>jazz</u> music. ⇒ _____

4. It takes <u>about ten minutes</u> to get to the station. ⇒ _____

5. I am <u>from Canada</u>. ⇒ _____

Task 2 語順に注意して、空所にそれぞれの語群から適切な単語を入れて文を完成させなさい。
文頭の語は最初の1字を大文字に変えること。

1. Can you tell _____ _____ a real flower?

is	which

2. I don't know _____ _____ _____ _____ _____ to the concert.

come	how	many	people	will

3. _____ _____ _____ _____ _____ win the mystery book award for this year?

do	think	you	who	will

4. _____ _____ _____ _____ _____ the actress is?

do	think	how	old	you

Try the TOEFL Test!

Task TOEFL テストの Section 2 形式の問題です。

Part A では空所に適切な語句を選び、Part B では A ～ D の下線部のうち間違っているものを選びなさい。

Part A: Structure

1. ------- do you think the death penalty issue has been so controversial?
   (A) Which
   (B) Why
   (C) That is
   (D) The reason why

   Ⓐ Ⓑ Ⓒ Ⓓ

2. Decades ago, ------ active volcanoes and strong earthquakes were concentrated in particular regions.
   (A) couldn't geologists explain why
   (B) why could geologists explain
   (C) geologists not explain why could
   (D) geologists could not explain why

   Ⓐ Ⓑ Ⓒ Ⓓ

Part B: Written Expression

1. Many scholars <u>have been analyzing</u> Shakespeare's plays and poems trying
              A

   <u>to dig out</u> <u>how to</u> he <u>lived</u> his life.
     B   **C**   **D**

   Ⓐ Ⓑ Ⓒ Ⓓ

2. <u>As</u> they consider arms <u>unimportant carry</u> out a <u>jumping</u> motion, some triple jumpers
    A   **B**   **C**

   <u>neglect to train</u> their upper body.
       D

   Ⓐ Ⓑ Ⓒ Ⓓ

3. In recent years, researchers have studied <u>how</u> molecules form crystals in the hope of
                            A

   better <u>understanding</u> <u>what types</u> of molecules and <u>whose conditions</u> will
         B   **C**   **D**

   distinguish unusual and useful molecular crystals from others.

   Ⓐ Ⓑ Ⓒ Ⓓ

4. Consider <u>how</u> it <u>used to take</u> to send mail across <u>a</u> comparatively short distance,
       A   **B**   **C**

   for example, in <u>the</u> 1600s it took two weeks to send mail from New York to Boston.
         D

   Ⓐ Ⓑ Ⓒ Ⓓ

Section 1
Listening Comprehension

 Track 19-23

In this section of the test, you will have an opportunity to demonstrate your ability to understand conversations and talks in English. There are three parts to this section with special directions for each part. Answer all the questions on the basis of what is stated or implied by the speakers you hear. Do **NOT** take notes or write in your test book at any time. Do **NOT** turn the pages until you are told to do so.

(**Part A**)

Directions: In Part A, you will hear short conversations between two people. After each conversation, you will hear a question about the conversation. The conversations and questions will not be repeated. After you hear a question, read the four possible answers in your test book and choose the best answer. Then, on your answer sheet, find the number of the question and fill in the space that corresponds to the letter of the answer you have chosen.

Here is an example.
On the recording, you will hear:

In your test book, you will read: (A) He doesn't like the painting either.
(B) He doesn't know how to paint.
(C) He doesn't have any paintings.
(D) He doesn't know what to do.

Sample Answer

You learn from the conversation that neither the man nor the woman likes the painting. The best answer to the question, "What does the man mean?" is (A), "He doesn't like the painting either." Therefore, the correct choice is (A).

1. (A) Renewing their contract.
   (B) Advertising on TV.
   (C) Contacting the woman.
   (D) Scheduling a meeting.
   Ⓐ Ⓑ Ⓒ Ⓓ

2. (A) His notes aren't very good.
   (B) There aren't any notes.
   (C) There was an assistant teacher.
   (D) The woman should take her own notes.
   Ⓐ Ⓑ Ⓒ Ⓓ

3. (A) The theater is closed.
   (B) She will see the film.
   (C) She is very busy.
   (D) The movie isn't interesting.
   Ⓐ Ⓑ Ⓒ Ⓓ

4. (A) Take care of children.
   (B) Play golf with friends.
   (C) Go shopping with the man.
   (D) Buy a present for the man.
   Ⓐ Ⓑ Ⓒ Ⓓ

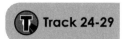
Directions: In this part, you will hear longer conversations. After each conversation, you will hear several questions. The conversations and questions will not be repeated.

After you hear a question, read the four possible answers in your test book and choose the best answer. Then, on your answer sheet, find the number of the question and fill in the space that corresponds to the letter of the answer you have chosen.

Remember, you are **NOT** allowed to take notes or write in your test book.

5. (A) Advisor.
(B) Professor.
(C) Student.
(D) Travel agent.
Ⓐ Ⓑ Ⓒ Ⓓ

6. (A) German.
(B) Science.
(C) Literature.
(D) History.
Ⓐ Ⓑ Ⓒ Ⓓ

7. (A) Less than half can enter.
(B) They all major in German.
(C) More than half are admitted.
(D) They must pass a language test.
Ⓐ Ⓑ Ⓒ Ⓓ

8. (A) Purchase tickets.
(B) Apply for studying abroad.
(C) Take an examination.
(D) Read pamphlets.
Ⓐ Ⓑ Ⓒ Ⓓ

(**Part C**)

Directions: In this part, you will hear several talks. After each talk, you will hear some questions. The talks and questions will not be repeated. After you hear a question, read the four possible answers in your test book and choose the best answer. Then, on your answer sheet, find the number of the question and fill in the space that corresponds to the letter of the answer you have chosen.

Here is an example.
On the recording, you will hear:

Now listen to a sample question.
In your test book, you will read: (A) To demonstrate the latest use of computer graphics. **Sample Answer**
(B) To discuss the possibility of an economic depression. Ⓐ Ⓑ ● Ⓓ
(C) To explain the workings of the brain.
(D) To dramatize a famous mystery story.

The best answer to the question, "What is the main purpose of the program?" is (C), "To explain the workings of the brain." Therefore, the correct choice is (C).

Now listen to another sample question.

In your test book, you will read: (A) It is required of all science majors.
(B) It will never be shown again.
(C) It can help viewers improve their memory skills.
(D) It will help with course work.

Sample Answer

Ⓐ Ⓑ Ⓒ ●

The best answer to the question, "Why does the speaker recommend watching the program?" is (D), "It will help with course work." Therefore, the correct choice is (D).

Remember, you are **NOT** allowed to take notes or write in your test book.

---

9. (A) To compare federalistic and democratic governments.
(B) To explain the structure of American federalism.
(C) To suggest how federalistic governments might change.
(D) To demonstrate that central governments are inefficient.

Ⓐ Ⓑ Ⓒ Ⓓ

10. (A) Running elections.
(B) Running the postal system.
(C) Printing money.
(D) Making international treaties.

Ⓐ Ⓑ Ⓒ Ⓓ

11. (A) Licenses.
(B) Elections.
(C) Courts.
(D) Health services.

Ⓐ Ⓑ Ⓒ Ⓓ

12. (A) It provides a balance of power.
(B) Other countries should adopt it.
(C) States will have more power.
(D) American citizens are not satisfied.

Ⓐ Ⓑ Ⓒ Ⓓ

Section 2
Structure and Written Expression
Time: 7 minutes

This section is designed to measure your ability to recognize language that is appropriate for standard written English. There are two types of questions in this section, with special directions for each type.

(Structure)

Directions: Questions 1-5 are incomplete sentences. Beneath each sentence you will see four words or phrases, marked (A), (B), (C), and (D). Choose the one word or phrase that best completes the sentence. Then, on your answer sheet, find the number of the question and fill in the space that corresponds to the letter of the answer you have chosen. Fill in the space so that the letter inside the oval cannot be seen.

Example I

Geysers have often been compared to volcanoes ------- they both emit hot liquids from below the Earth's surface.

(A) due to   (C) in spite of   **Sample Answer**

(B) because   (D) regardless of

The sentence should read, "Geysers have often been compared to volcanoes because they both emit hot liquids from below the Earth's surface." Therefore, you should choose answer (B).

Example II

During the early period of ocean navigation, ------- any need for sophisticated instruments and techniques.

(A) so that hardly   (C) hardly was   **Sample Answer**

(B) where there hardly was   (D) there was hardly

The sentence should read, "During the early period of ocean navigation, there was hardly any need for sophisticated instruments and techniques." Therefore, you should choose answer (D).

Now begin work on the questions.

---

1. Language learning experiences ------- to prevent some brain diseases.
   (A) have proven
   (B) proves
   (C) proving
   (D) has proven

2. ------- influenza is that it increases our awareness of hygiene.
   (A) Among the hazards of
   (B) According to the main list
   (C) Because of the numerous difficulties
   (D) The best that can be said about

3. The reason we chose ------- by train is the substantial time it would have taken compared to driving.
   (A) have gone
   (B) to go
   (C) not to go
   (D) would have gone

4. Mark Twain is the man ------- is considered the father of American literature.
   (A) whose
   (B) who
   (C) whoever
   (D) whom

5. Police officers ------- to stop drivers but not to arrest them without a good reason.
   (A) can power
   (B) to the power
   (C) have the power
   (D) is powerful

Written Expression

Directions: In questions 6-10 each sentence has four underlined words or phrases. The four underlined parts of the sentence are marked (A), (B), (C), and (D). Identify the one underlined word or phrase that must be changed in order for the sentence to be correct. Then, on your answer sheet, find the number of the question and fill in the space that corresponds to the letter of the answer you have chosen.

Example I

Guppies are sometimes <u>call</u> rainbow <u>fish</u> <u>because</u> of the males' <u>bright</u> colors.
                  A   **B**   **C**   **D**

Sample Answer
● Ⓑ Ⓒ Ⓓ

The sentence should read, "Guppies are sometimes called rainbow fish because of the males' bright colors." Therefore, you should choose answer (A).

Example II

<u>Serving</u> several <u>term</u> in Congress, Shirley Chisholm became an <u>important</u>
   A   **B**   **C**

Sample Answer
Ⓐ ● Ⓒ Ⓓ

United States <u>politician</u>.
          D

The sentence should read, "Serving several terms in Congress, Shirley Chisholm became an important United States politician." Therefore, you should choose answer (B).

Now begin work on the questions.

---

6. A classmate of <u>myself</u> said <u>that</u> the mid-term essay will <u>account for</u> 30% of the final
                   A   **B**   **C**   Ⓐ Ⓑ Ⓒ Ⓓ

<u>grade</u>.
   D

7. <u>Although</u> running for office is an exhausting <u>endeavor</u>, <u>win</u> an election is very
    A   **B**   **C**

<u>satisfying</u>.
   D   Ⓐ Ⓑ Ⓒ Ⓓ

8. If you're not sure about <u>when</u> to do after <u>graduating</u>, you <u>should</u> see a career counselor.
  A   **B**   **C**   **D**   Ⓐ Ⓑ Ⓒ Ⓓ

9. Professor Smith <u>requires</u> that his students <u>read</u> over 3,000 pages <u>any</u> <u>semester</u>.
                   A   **B**   **C**   **D**   Ⓐ Ⓑ Ⓒ Ⓓ

10. Believe it or not, studying literature <u>lead</u> to a <u>variety</u> of <u>unexpected</u> <u>careers</u>.
                         A   **B**   **C**   **D**   Ⓐ Ⓑ Ⓒ Ⓓ

Section 3
Reading Comprehension
Time: 10 minutes

Directions: In this section you will read several passages. Each one is followed by several questions about it. For questions 1-10, you are to choose the one best answer, (A), (B), (C), or (D), to each question. Then, on your answer sheet, find the number of the question and fill in the space that corresponds to the letter of the answer you have chosen. Answer all questions following a passage on the basis of what is stated or implied in that passage.

Read the following passage:

> The railroad was not the first institution to impose regularity on society, or to draw attention to the importance of precise timekeeping. For as long as merchants have set out their wares at daybreak and communal festivities have been celebrated, people have been in rough agreement with their neighbors as to the time of day. The value of this tradition is today more apparent than ever. Were it not for public acceptance of a single yardstick of time, social life $\quad$ *5* would be unbearably chaotic: the massive daily transfers of goods, services, and information would proceed in fits and starts; the very fabric of modern society would begin to unravel.

Example I

What is the main idea of the passage?

Sample Answer

(A) In modern society we must make more time for our neighbors.

Ⓐ Ⓑ ● Ⓓ

(B) The traditions of society are timeless.

(C) An accepted way of measuring time is essential for the smooth functioning of society.

(D) Society judges people by the times at which they conduct certain activities.

The main idea of the passage is that societies need to agree about how time is to be measured in order to function smoothly. Therefore, you should choose answer (C).

Example II

In line 4, the phrase "this tradition" refers to

Sample Answer

(A) the practice of starting the business day at dawn

(B) friendly relations between neighbors

(C) the railroad's reliance on time schedules

(D) people's agreement on the measurement of time

The phrase "this tradition" refers to the preceding clause, "people have been in rough agreement with their neighbors as to the time of day." Therefore, you should choose answer (D).

Now begin work on the questions.

Questions 1-10

Sinkholes, as their name implies, are holes of varying sizes where earth has sunk lower than the surrounding ground. A typical reason for their formation is the gradual removal of sedimentary rock (made up of many smaller particles) such as limestone, chalk, dolostone, sandstone, conglomerate, some types of breccia, and shale by penetrating water. A second way sinkholes can be formed is when the roof of an *5* underlying cave suddenly collapses and yet another is when the water level lowers which removes the supporting characteristics of the liquid and causes weaker earth to fall inward.

By and large, sinkholes are made by the forces of nature. The gradual removal of rock is most often caused by rainwater falling for thousands upon thousands of years *10* and steadily percolating past layers of topsoil and into the porous bedrock (a solid rock layer). Water then seeps between coarser particles in the bedrock and washes away smaller ones that bind the rock together causing the bedrock to disintegrate.

Sinkholes can also be partially formed from forces below the surface of Earth. Occasionally, subterranean (below the surface) streams with relatively high rates of flow *15* can carve out bedrock itself, creating a cavern in the process. Rainwater seeping from the surface does the rest of the work in weakening the top of the structure leading to a collapse. One extraordinary sample of this is Cedar Sink in Mammoth Cave National Park in the U.S.A., which amazingly has a river flowing across the sinkhole's floor.

On the other hand, sinkholes can also be a result of human activities, namely *20* land-use practices. For example, they can be formed when groundwater is pumped to the surface which leaves an unsupported cavern in its place. They can also be formed when natural surface water drainage patterns are changed and water diversion systems are developed, which change the delicate supportive balance between water and bedrock. Still another way humans can inadvertently create sinkholes is when land features such as *25* ponds are created. The weight of these new features can set off a collapse of supporting material which causes a sinkhole. In manipulating land for their own use, humans can ruin farmland if they are not careful about unintentionally creating sinkholes.

1. What is the author's main focus about sinkholes?
   (A) Their locations
   (B) Their use by humans
   (C) Their natural effects
   (D) Their formation
   Ⓐ Ⓑ Ⓒ Ⓓ

2. The word "gradual" in line 3 is closest in meaning to
   (A) surprising
   (B) sudden
   (C) swift
   (D) steady
   Ⓐ Ⓑ Ⓒ Ⓓ

3. Where in the passage does the author provide a term for "underground"?
   (A) Line 21
   (B) Line 15
   (C) Line 3
   (D) Line 11
   Ⓐ Ⓑ Ⓒ Ⓓ

4. According to the passage, how does percolation function in making sinkholes?
   (A) Topsoil holds water until underlying bedrock is weakened.
   (B) Features such as ponds weigh heavily on the ground.
   (C) Water removes smaller rock pieces weakening bedrock.
   (D) Flowing underground water eats away at bedrock making a cave.
   Ⓐ Ⓑ Ⓒ Ⓓ

5. The word "disintegrate" in line 13 is closest in meaning to
   (A) break up
   (B) transform
   (C) rise up
   (D) attach
   Ⓐ Ⓑ Ⓒ Ⓓ

6. The word "seeping" in line 16 is closest in meaning to
   (A) returning
   (B) leaking
   (C) drying
   (D) collecting
   Ⓐ Ⓑ Ⓒ Ⓓ

7. In which paragraph does the author use an actual example of a sinkhole?
   (A) One
   (B) Two
   (C) Three
   (D) Four
   Ⓐ Ⓑ Ⓒ Ⓓ

8. Which is NOT mentioned as a natural reason for sinkhole formation?
   (A) Varying levels of buried water
   (B) Underground rivers making caves
   (C) Rainwater filtering through bedrock
   (D) Earthquakes destabilizing the ground
   Ⓐ Ⓑ Ⓒ Ⓓ

9. The word "inadvertently" in line 25 is closest in meaning to
   (A) beneficially
   (B) accidentally
   (C) tragically
   (D) purposefully
   Ⓐ Ⓑ Ⓒ Ⓓ

10. What does the author imply about man-made sinkholes?
    (A) They do damage to the environment.
    (B) They are often located in urban settings.
    (C) They are sometimes created purposefully.
    (D) They hold water for farming irrigation.
    Ⓐ Ⓑ Ⓒ Ⓓ

教師用音声CD有り（非売品）　**クラス用音声CD有り（非売品）**

Power-up Trainer for the TOEFL® ITP [Text Only]

2010年1月20日　初版発行
2023年2月10日　Text Only版第1刷

著者　　　Mark D.Stafford ／ 妻鳥千鶴子
発行　　　センゲージ ラーニング株式会社
　　　　　〒102-0073　東京都千代田区九段北1-11-11 第2フナトビル5階
　　　　　電話　　03-3511-4392
　　　　　FAX　　03-3511-4391
　　　　　e-mail: eltjapan@cengage.com

　　　　　株式会社アスク出版
　　　　　〒162-8558　東京都新宿区下宮比町2-6

制作　　　株式会社アスク出版

装丁／本文デザイン　（株）アスク　デザイン部
イラスト　　　　　　しものともひろ
組版　　　　　　　　つむらともこ

ISBN 978-4-86312-417-2